Process and Dipolar Reality

Process and Dipolar Reality

An Essay in Process, Event Metaphysics
Rethinking Whitehead's Categoreal Scheme

DUANE VOSKUIL

WIPF & STOCK · Eugene, Oregon

PROCESS AND DIPOLAR REALITY
An Essay in Process, Event Metaphysics Rethinking Whitehead's Categoreal Scheme

Copyright © 2016 Duane Voskuil. All rights reserved. Except for brief quotations in critical publications or reviews, no part of this book may be reproduced in any manner without prior written permission from the publisher. Write: Permissions, Wipf and Stock Publishers, 199 W. 8th Ave., Suite 3, Eugene, OR 97401.

Wipf & Stock
An Imprint of Wipf and Stock Publishers
199 W. 8th Ave., Suite 3
Eugene, OR 97401

www.wipfandstock.com

ISBN 13: 978-1-62564-197-7

Manufactured in the U.S.A.   01/06/2016

To all those who know the importance and excitement of seeking concepts that set the ultimate context of meaning for everything.

Philosophy will not regain its proper status until the gradual elaboration of categoreal schemes, definitely stated at each stage of progress, is recognized as its proper objective ... Metaphysical categories are not dogmatic statements of the obvious; they are tentative formulations of the ultimate generalities.

Alfred North Whitehead, *Process and Reality*, 8

Thus the ultimacy of dualities does not validate dualism. There can be an all-inclusive form of reality, within which every contrast falls. After all, a whole contrasts with its parts, yet "the whole and its parts" is not more than the whole.

Charles Hartshorne, *Creative Synthesis and Philosophic Method*, 90

Contents

Preface: Why this Proposal for a New Categoreal Scheme | ix
Acknowledgments | xiii
Introduction: Some Procedural Observations | xv
Abbreviations | xx

Chapter 1
Rethinking the Categoreal Scheme | 1

Chapter 2
The Categoreal Scheme | 5

Chapter 3
Metaphysics and Change: Principles of Epochal Universality | 36

Chapter 4
Basic Anatomy of an Actual Entity: Discussion of the Dipolar Epochal Categories | 40

Chapter 5
Comparing Whitehead's Categoreal Obligations | 57

Chapter 6
The Necessarily Existing Society of Perspectival Occasions: Minimally Creative Processes | 64

Chapter 7
The Necessarily Existing Society of Non-Perspectival Occasions: Maximally Creative Processes | 73

Chapter 8
Necessary, Coordinate Contrasts within Process Wholes | 92

Chapter 9
Necessary, Sequential Contrasts within Process Wholes | 97

Chapter 10
Birth and Death of Hierarchal Relationships | 101

Chapter 11
Movement within Non-Moving Wholes | 112

Chapter 12
Entanglement's Challenge to Metaphysics | 126

Chapter 13
Presentational Immediacy | 132

Appendix: The Bare Categoreal Scheme | 135

Works Cited | 143
Index | 145

Preface

Why this Proposal for a New Categoreal Scheme

FIFTY YEARS HAVE PASSED since I first studied Alfred North Whitehead and Charles Hartshorne under Hartshorne at Emory University. Decades since studying their primary sources left me awed at what they accomplished. But for at least the last twenty years I've become increasing dissatisfied with the structure and clarity of Whitehead's Categoreal Scheme. I've also wanted to incorporate Hartshorne's views, particularly his theory of potentiality as a continuum (first expressed in his insightful book, *The Philosophy and Psychology of Sensation*, 1934) and his analysis of theism as a personal society, something that always made more sense to me than assuming divinity to be one actuality enduring through time, an exception to Whitehead's own insight that change implies a series of wholes, each one subsuming prior wholes' accomplishments as parts allowing the comparison of earlier to later fixed states, i.e., change.

A common theme throughout their work is an emphasis on dipolar wholes, that is, wholes incorporating and contrasting with their parts. Yet, as important as dipolarity is as a fundamental concept it must always be supplemented with the momentariness of events: All wholes (that is, subjects or process units), all cease processing after a finite life span.

Whitehead formulates some of his Categories as dipolarities, for instance, Categoreal Obligation, ix, Freedom and Determination: The "final decision is the reaction of the unity of the *whole* to its own internal determination [*parts*]" (PR 28, emphasis added). The Category of the Ultimate itself, "The many become one and are increased by one," is also dipolar, though unfortunately expressed in "one-many," rather than "part-whole," language. The "one-many" language allows of two interpretations depending on whether the "one" refers to "one process" or "one determinate being," that is, one processing whole or one determinate part (all determinations must be parts in some whole or other). Such ambiguity at this most basic level can change the meaning of much of the Categoreal System as I first pointed out in, "Disassembling the Mantra: Part/Whole Equivocation in the Category of the Ultimate," *Process Studies*, 2001.

Process philosophy explicitly eschews dualisms, supposedly replacing them with dipolarities, though not always successfully: Note the two "fundamentals" in Whitehead's Category of Explanation, xix, "the [two] fundamental types of entities are actual entities, and eternal objects..." (PR 25). Whitehead never makes clear why this is not a dualism.

The clearest way to state "dipolarities" is to use the "whole-part" concept. The subject-object language is also ambiguous since a common historical theme (in substance philosophies) has allowed subjects to have multiple adventures, to have a succession of different experiences and remain the same subject.

So, I set out many years ago to find a way to express all the Categories dipolarly. The Categoreal Obligations lent themselves to dipolar formulations, expressing how wholes are "obliged" to process as they carry the past as internal, determinate parts and then become parts themselves for successive wholes. Whitehead did not call the Categories of Explanation, Obligations; yet many seem to be descriptions of how actual entities either must behave or may behave, for example, Category of Explanation, xvii, "Thus the many components [parts] of a complex datum have a unity [wholeness]: this unity is a 'contrast' of entities [parts]" (PR 24). All contrasts can only be simultaneous comparisons of parts in a whole, by a whole, that extends over the parts simultaneously even if they occurred successively.

Whitehead failed to keep clearly separated the "must" from the "may," the metaphysical from the merely cosmological conditions. This is not just true of the Categories of Explanation, but also of the Categoreal Obligations, where Transmutation is a condition that can only be found in higher-level occasions that need not exist.

While working on restating the Scheme to be thoroughly and obviously dipolar and metaphysically universal, it become clear that there is a modal difference between the society of actual entities that is the universe and the societies of actual entities that are in the universe. These differences are not differences of chance or choice (something that makes every actual entity unique), but are unavoidable, necessary differences. Insofar as Whitehead addresses these, they tend to be afterthoughts, but I eventually found that they must be an integral part of the Categoreal Scheme itself, as must be every unavoidable or necessary aspect. As Hartshorne would say, either the universe is unavoidably "theistic" or impossibly so: The rationale for an all-inclusive, necessarily existing personal society is as fundamental to the Categoreal Scheme as is the meaning of an "actual entity" itself.

But upon further consideration the modal distinction between the necessarily existing, cosmic personal society and the contingently existing societies of actual occasions of the world, is too simpleminded. Even though all actual entities are contingent, and even though the cosmic society of actual entities is necessary, and even though worldly societies of actual occasions exist contingently, still some worldly society or other is necessary, because without new data at the initiation of each dipolar, cosmic Whole, the cosmic Wholes could not occur.

Finally, there are Whitehead's Categories of Entity Types, or Categories of Existence. How can they be expressed as dipolar conditions? All entities, except *actualizing* entities, are aspects or parts of actual entities. Even actual entities, when they cease as "actualizing" processes, become determinate parts of successive actualizing wholes. So there really is only one type: actual entities: All other entities are really "parts" or characteristics of actual entities.

If the "part" is an actual entity's satisfaction-superject (a being that has come to be), it exists only as a part in successive processing-wholes. Anything said about the being will be a characteristic of it; it will be an aspect of the actualized entities, that is, an abstraction. If it is an unavoidable aspect, a characteristic that every being must exhibit, it is a metaphysically general abstraction and, as such, must find its place in the Categoreal Scheme.

During my journey to redo the Scheme, I've faced other concerns, such as, what does Whitehead mean by "negative prehensions;" I've finally concluded that only beings not prior and contiguous to a nascent actual entity are not experienced; otherwise, all nascent actual entities must take in as parts all those, and all of each, that lie within the scope of its "spatial" volume, namely, all those beings it overlaps. One of these beings will be "privileged," that is, the immediate termination of a prior process.

Finally, I was forced, and very uncomfortably so, to give up the "pre-established harmony" Whitehead refers to in Categoreal Obligation i (and vii):

> The many feelings which belong to an incomplete phase in the process of an actual entity, though unintegrated by reason of the

Preface

> incompleteness of the phase, are compatible for integration by reason of the unity of their subject (*PR* 26).

Given the definition of a "privileged" being, along with maintaining the truth of Categoreal Obligation i, death of a personal society seems impossible. This is all well and good for the Unsurpassable Personal Society, and maybe even true for personal strands in the least complex, non-personal society, but contingently existing personal societies must have had a first member and will have a last. I have concluded that some actual occasions must begin but not reach a satisfaction.

I offer the following Categoreal Scheme as a "gradual elaboration," hopefully clearly and "definitely stated" so as to be eligible as a "stage of progress" in the continuing effort to fulfill philosophy's "proper objective" (*PR* 8).

Acknowledgments

QUOTATIONS ARE REPRINTED WITH permission of Scribner Publishing Group a division of Simon & Schuster, Inc. from *Process and Reality* by Alfred North Whitehead. Copyright © 1929 by The Macmillan Company: copyright renewed © 1967 by Evelyn Whitehead. Copyright © 1978 by Free Press, a division of Simon and Schuster, Inc. All rights reserved.

Quotations are reprinted with permission of Scribner Publishing Group a division of Simon & Schuster, Inc. from *Adventures of Ideas* by Alfred North Whitehead. Copyright © 1933 by The Macmillan Company: copyright renewed © 1961 by Evelyn Whitehead. All rights reserved.

Introduction
Some Procedural Observations

PHILOSOPHY AIMS TO EXPLAIN. Amongst its tasks is the aim to explain what "explanation" means and how philosophical explanation is alike and different from other forms. Any attempt to explain presumes a conceptual context, yet the most adequate context can only come, if at all, at the end of a systematic attempt to explain what the universal context is. Such is the radical nature of a discipline that differs from all other forms of explanation by its unlimited scope. Since philosophical explanation must even explain what "philosophy" is, disagreements on what the task of philosophy is are inevitable.

Coming to an awareness of one's unarticulated assumptions and what necessarily follows from holding them, is the process of philosophical inquiry. Every effort must be made to allow all possible approaches to have a hearing. The faith that drives every metaphysician is that when all attempts to explain have been examined, one and only one will survive (assuming it articulates reality as it necessarily is). All others will not be (should not be) rejected because they differ from the lone survivor, but each will fail because something within the proposed contender was itself inconsistent or inadequate to explain what it attempted to explain. The faith, in other words, is that reality is not irrational and only one explanation can do justice to what is unrestrictively rational, unless analysis establishes two or more proposals to be equivalent.

Explanation also requires clarity of expression. A vague or ambivalent attempt to explain may survive the test of obvious inconsistency or inadequacy, but it pays a price not obvious until the various ways of removing the vagueness are articulated. Schisms are born, often with painful social consequences, with one side of a split emphasizing one aspect of a complex truth, while the other side embraces another. Either–or mentality dominates.

Yet, because the clarity obtained by removing the vagueness often fails to account for truth left out, there is movement towards synthesis, a movement to reconcile the polarization within a new scheme. The challenge then is to provide an explanation that is not merely a juxtaposition of conflicting ideas, but one wherein the ideas are compatible contrasts necessarily requiring and reinforcing the truth of each other. Such is the goal of *dipolar* explanations.

Explanations are abstract. Just what an "abstraction" is, therefore, has been a major philosophical issue, and one that can only be fully resolved at the end of a systematic examination, if then. However, everyone has some grasp of the difference between what is concrete and what is abstract. Even though the final or most adequate explanation may reinterpret what seems to be the most concretely real, still we know the difference between a mother and motherhood, between what is the case and what could have been. The world is as it is, and explanations are either descriptions of how it came to be, in part, as it is (empirical science) or why it must be, in part, as it is (metaphysics).

The intuited world as it concretely presents itself to us is not simple. But the world, as explained, should be. Not "simple" as in "easy to understand," but simple as in one abstraction must apply to all that is explained or something is not explained. Historically, explanations have proposed that reality is either composed of many concrete things or just one concrete thing. When reality is seen as many, there is often a failure to explain how the many are together in one reality. On the other hand, declaring reality to be concretely one, requires explaining why and how we experience diversity. The ancient problem of the One and the Many is always with us.

Since philosophy's explanations differ from other disciplines in trying to explain "everything," not just some things, no concrete item can be an exception to its final explanation. It is not, however, or should not be, the attempt to say everything about everything. It is only the attempt to say something about everything, to point out how every possible concrete thing must be alike in some ways despite their necessary differences. Philosophical explanation strives to be necessary, to express what is unavoidable, not because it is defined to be, but because any attempt to discuss anything without explicitly or implicitly evoking its explanation must fail.

Introduction

Some philosophers have indeed declared the concrete universe to be just as it is because everything about it is necessary. Their position, known as "ultra-rationalism" or "complete determinism," does imply that everything about everything concrete is knowable. Such a definition of "explanation" denies any freedom to create, since either change is not real or what results from a change is, supposedly, fully knowable (as is) before it happens.

Other philosophers deny there is anything that every concrete item must have in common with all others. They declare all so-called necessary unavoidables are only definitions that could be defined otherwise. Ultra-rationalism and relativism are likely half-truths waiting to be reconciled.

The Categoreal Scheme that follows assumes there are truths that are not made up, not merely definitional. These are truths about reality that are to be discovered and, given adequate insight, cannot be avoided because they express how reality is and must be, *in part*. Yet, there are other truths that express some characteristics reality exhibits in its full concreteness. These are truths that describe how things happen to be, in addition to how they must be.

There are truths, therefore, that express what everything must have in common just to be anything at all; and there are truths that express how a thing in its fullness differs from others, actual or possible. Relativism is right to emphasize the differences all actual things *must* have from each other; yet rationalism is right to insist that there must be something all differences have in common. Even that all acts must be different from all other acts is at least one (abstract) thing all (concrete) things have in common.

Explanation not only seeks to find common threads differences exhibit, it also seeks to classify these threads into more and more general classes—ending only when all find a place within one class or Category so general no actual or possible thing is left out. This Ultimate Category is necessary and unavoidable since only "nothingness" could be an exception, but "nothingness" is not a possible state of affairs that can be an alternative to something. A danger exists that this universal, abstract class will not be seen as abstract, but as concrete, as the one "stuff" that everything is made of.

We intuitively know that abstractions can't be that which makes reality concrete, much less one *universe*. Abstractions are parts or aspects of (concrete) wholes. If the concrete wholeness of reality cannot reside in an abstraction, maybe, some assert, a concrete stuff that is the same stuff everywhere at all times can be that which holds everything together as one reality. This "concrete universal" is both the biggest mistake philosophers have made and yet close to the most important insight that a philosopher can make.

Since nothing concrete can change, being what it is and then being something other than what it is, the so-called concrete universal would be the most paradoxically changing thing—changing when anything changes, and yet somehow always remaining the same (concrete) thing. This contradiction, first pointed out by Parmenides (ca. 500 BCE) still has force. But the intellectual and emotional need to find the unity of concrete reality is so strong most will live with this pantheistic contradiction rather than deny reality is a *uni*verse.

Philosophy, as Whitehead said, should seek simplicity but distrust it, and the simplicity of pantheism's concrete universal gives good reason to be leery, but the nominalism of conceptualism is also a retreat from finding an explanation of concrete wholeness. Some Buddhists' and Whitehead's insight that concrete wholeness is momentary is the key to reconciling the abstract necessities and concrete contingencies.

Necessities are patterns all contingencies exhibit. For example, nothing exists without exhibiting a modal status. Things never just are: they are, but could have been otherwise, or they are and could not have been otherwise. Every whole or concrete moment of reality could have been somewhat otherwise from the way it is; but every whole exhibits characteristics that could not have been otherwise, namely, what it means to be a "whole."

Dipolar explanations see opposites like freedom and determinism as aspects that every fully real, concrete moment exhibits. Freedom and determinateness are both aspects of a whole, but not aspects on equal footing. One side of a dipolar contrast is the inclusive pole: It characterizes the whole. The other side is the included pole: It characterizes the parts in a whole. A whole as a whole could not be fully determined while even one part remains free. However, a whole as a whole could be free to do or become various things and yet have parts or aspects of itself that are not free to be different from the way they are.

So, if freedom and determinism are to reside together in a concrete reality, freedom must be a characteristic of the whole that is conditioned or determined by its parts, though never exhaustively so. If the whole were nothing in addition to "its" parts, it would not be an "it" at all. Wholes can only exist if they are more than their parts. This more is at least the simultaneous inclusion of all the parts, providing an experience of the relationships the parts have to each other. The whole also has the power to add something somewhat new to its parts, despite the necessity for the past to be determinate and changeless within the whole. Charles Hartshorne has expressed this *principle of inclusive contrast* or dipolarity well:

> Thus the ultimacy of dualities does not validate dualism. There can be an all-inclusive form of reality, within which every contrast falls. After all, a whole contrasts with its parts, yet "the whole and its parts" is not more than the whole (*CSPM* 90).

The Categoreal Scheme is the attempt to be as explicit as possible on the most fundamental assumptions proposed for the metaphysic. Baldly stated they are hard to understand since they give little help in moving from previous understandings to new insights. Such a move depends on metaphors describing what the new Categories have in common with old patterns and how they differ. Such metaphors push language to the limit by using old words in new ways that require an effort on the reader's part to gain a new insight.

Abbreviations

AD   *Anselm's Discovery: A Re-Examination of the Ontological Proof for God's Existence*, Charles Hartshorne.

AI   *Adventures of Ideas*, Alfred North Whitehead.

CSPM *Creative Synthesis and Philosophic Method*, Charles Hartshorne.

MT   *Modes of Thought*, Alfred North Whitehead.

PR   *Process and Reality: An Essay in Cosmology*, Alfred North Whitehead.

Chapter 1

Rethinking the Categoreal Scheme

> [S]ubjective experience is the primary metaphysical situation . . . [and] Any instance of experience is dipolar, whether that instance be God or an actual occasion of the world (*PR* 160 and 36).
>
> The metaphysical characteristics of an actual entity—in the proper general sense of "metaphysics"—should be those which apply to all actual entities (*PR* 90).
>
> The most general sense of the meaning of change is "the differences between actual occasions in one event" (*PR* 80).

For a rational scheme to exhibit coherence, there must be one principle providing the ultimate context of meaning for all other principles: It must be a single proposition so general that every other proposition will be a further specification of what it means. The Category of the *Ultimate* expresses this conceptual unity by expressing the necessity for every moment of reality to be a whole, simultaneously extending over others' actualizations as its parts, a dipolar whole whose existence is temporally finite, and when it ceases with its own accomplishment, it ceases being a whole and is immediately one part, the "privileged" part, of many parts in a new whole. There are three Categoreal subgroups providing more detail.

The first type expresses the dipolar, *Epochal* foundation *every* moment must exhibit in the same way with no exceptions. The term "epochal" follows Whitehead by referring to the atomistic and cyclical nature of temporal extension every actual entity has: birth, growth, and death, only to have other superseding actualities repeat the cycle. It also refers to the unique set of determinate parts each whole simultaneously includes as its spatial location. Used here, "epochal" refers to all the unavoidable conditions every process "atom" must exhibit.

> In respect to time, this atomization takes the special form of the 'epochal theory of time.' In respect to space, it means that every actual entity in the temporal world is to be credited with a spatial volume for its perspective standpoint . . . The authority of William James can be quoted in support of this conclusion. He writes: "Either your experience is of no content, of no change, or it is of a perceptible amount of content or change. Your acquaintance with reality grows literally by buds or drops of perception" (PR 68).

The epochal principles are the conditions every whole must exhibit, from the greatest to the least significant actual entity conceivable. All, for example, have a finite temporal lifespan and must inherit (many) others' accomplishments simultaneously as it begins.

There is no set number of epochal principles since the dipolar nature of reality can be expressed in many ways depending on one's focus and the language used. Even though Whitehead seems rather dogmatic in stating how many Categories there are of each kind, he also says, "Each actual entity is analysable in an indefinite number of ways" (PR 19); I propose this analysis extends to an indefinite number of ways metaphysical necessities can be expressed. Fully expressed, the thirteen epochal subcategories suggested here would be seen as synonyms of each other.

The second sub-group, *Modal* contrasts, expresses the dipolarity between supreme (or non-perspectival) and fragmentary (or perspectival) actualities, that is, contrasts exhibited at an actual entity's birth and throughout its creative growth. Modal principles describe the origin of new content and its comparative value. At each moment there must be one all-inclusive, supreme fulfillment of the metaphysical principles, and many fragmentary exemplifications. Every fragmentary accomplishment and each supreme Whole's termination is a part in the next supreme Whole. A "whole" refers both to the temporal extension an actual entity requires to create a new determination (that is, the process from its inception to its perishing as a datum for successive others) and to its spatial extension (that is, the simultaneous inclusion of others' accomplishments). An actual entity's satisfaction is never a whole; it is a datum that is always a part within successive others.

The third type, *Social* contrasts, expresses the necessary relationships actualities have to each other and the necessary contrasts they generate and must exhibit at all levels. Every whole unavoidably exhibits a dipolar contrast between its parts and the whole process in which they are parts (as expressed by the Epochal categories), but the emphasis in this group is on how wholes, or more precisely, former wholes, must be organized spatially and temporally, that is, how they are related to each other externally and internally.

Wholes may employ additional *contingent* principles to make the most of their creative power. Even cosmic Wholes, that always exhibit creative power supremely, must at each moment contingently create one determination within a continuum of coequally valuable possibilities for that moment. Though not metaphysically necessary, the many forms of contrasts and contrasts of contrasts, which can be contingently created, are of much interest in coming to understand the origin of cosmological species. Much of Whitehead's work on the Theory of Prehension, including his Categoreal Obligation, Transmutation, is a cosmological analysis, not one of metaphysical generality. An effort will be made in the following chapters to maintain a clear distinction between principles purporting to be absolutely unavoidable and those that are contingent.

In short, there must be principles (1) that express what it means to be a concrete reality of any kind (the Ultimate and Epochal categories), (2) principles that distinguish realities from each other by quantitative and qualitative capacity (the Modal categories), and (3) principles that express the kinds of relationships realities must and may have with each other (the Social categories).

In the scheme presented here, every fundamental reality, every concrete act of existence, begins and ends. It is a temporal *epoch* of some finite duration that begins by building upon, or around, others and ends, if it is successful, as a part in others' creative growths.

A moment of reality is not merely an undifferentiated duration. Every moment "feels" the past and strives to accomplish new concrete value to pass on to others. This effort may end, (a) with its accomplishment unsurpassed up to that moment (a creation that could not have been better at that moment, though it could have been equaled), (b) satisfied with an accomplishment that is limited both in quantitative scope and qualitative excellence due to its unavoidable perspective and limited creative ability, or (c) unfulfilled in any way since the inherited, generic conditions were in the end too chaotic for the nascent actual occasion to succeed in its effort to create a newly specified determination.

In what follows, "actual entity" and "moment" will be understood to refer to both supreme (unsurpassed)[1] and fragmentary (surpassed) actualities, whereas "occasion" will only refer to fragmentary actualities. The necessity for reality to exhibit the contrast of necessity-within-contingency and fragmentariness-within-all-inclusiveness, both with their contrasting degrees of excellence, is the unavoidable *modal* dipolarity of reality.

Both Epochal and Modal characteristics are implied in the Category of the Ultimate (the Ultimate Dipolar Principle) and exhibited by the *societies* that actual*ized* wholes exhibit in their necessary relationships to each other. Societies also exhibit contingently created, determinate accomplishments that exist as parts of new wholes, parts that are simultaneously contrasting with each other either as mutually externally connected or as parts internally connected to others external to them.[2] Again, determinate beings will be experienced as next to and outside each other or as parts within a being including them. These relationships form societies that exhibit both their contingent creations and the Categoreal necessities.

The necessity for reality to exhibit dipolarity means every part, in being a part, implies a whole containing the part. Likewise, every whole must inherit some determinate parts or other. Any discussion of a whole apart from its parts or of parts apart from the whole they are in is an analysis abstracting from a whole; it leaves something out. Though such analyses can be valuable, care must be taken to avoid committing the Fallacy of Misplaced Concreteness, as Whitehead calls it, by forgetting that other aspects of the dipolar relationship are always, necessarily, aspects of the full reality under analysis.

---

1. Cosmic actual entities are unsurpassed (at the time they are creating), but every actual entity is surpassable. "Unsurpassabiity" can only be a property of a personal society of actual entities wherein each unsurpassed Whole is surpassed unsurpassably by the next, following Whole.

2. Care must be taken as to how "internal" and "external" are used. In "part-whole" language a part is "in" the whole, but in the language of relations, the part is external to the whole because it is unaffected by what the whole is or does.

Chapter 2

The Categoreal Scheme

THE CATEGORY OF THE Ultimate Dipolarity and the three types of metaphysical sub-Categories are:

1. The Category of Ultimate Dipolarity
2. Categories of Dipolar Epochal Universality
3. Categories of Dipolar Modal Contrasts
4. Categories of Entity Types and Societal Organization

The Category of the Ultimate and each of the Epochal categories are expressed as dipolar contrasts in themselves; however, each of the Modal categories state only one side of a modal dipolarity, namely, either the supreme, unsurpassed pole or the fragmentary, surpassed pole. The modal dipolarity arises because the non-supreme, fragmentary occasions create parts to be included in the all-inclusive, supreme Wholes. Modal status is an unavoidable addition to an actual entity's Epochal characteristics. The Societal contrasts of momentary actualized entities concerns how groups of satisfied entities survive organized as the subordinate pole of successive dipolar actualities.

In the following elaboration of the Categories the quotations in braces are mostly from Whitehead's Categoreal Scheme, *Process and Reality*, part 1, chapter 2, that are similar to, or different from, the Categoreal proposals set out here. An attempt has been made to include (but not be restricted to) all of Whitehead's Categories either by agreeing or disagreeing with them. Despite placing the Categories near the beginning of this essay (following

Whitehead's example), they really are as much a summary of the discussion to follow, and can be skipped if they are too tedious upon the first reading.

SECTION 1: THE ULTIMATE PRINCIPLE

U: The Category of the Ultimate Dipolarity between a Whole and Its Parts—Each of many wholes *that comes to be* is a part in successive wholes. {The Category of the Ultimate: "The many become one, and are increased by one" *PR* 21.}

> **U1: Societal Longevity**—Sequentially Many: Every whole that comes to be is a changeless part in successive wholes forever.
>
> **U2: Societal Inclusiveness**—Coordinately Many: Every whole that comes to be includes some or all of those that have come to be.
>
> **U3: Process' Determination as a Privileged Beginning**—Unique One of Many: Every whole that comes to be is a privileged part in its immediately successive whole.

An actual entity can only reach a satisfaction as a part in a new actual entity since a determinate being can only exist as determining process. The satisfied determination is immediately a datum for one[3] "privileged" successor that also embraces, as it begins, all other beings contiguous to it. These additional, non-privileged beings are sustained by other actual entities whose processes inherited these beings (as privileged for them) just prior to the initiation of the actual entity in question that began with the datum privileged for it.

> **U4: Process Determinations as Qualitatively Diverse Values**—Many Values, One Unique—Every whole in striving to come to be, either fails, happens to succeed, or necessarily succeeds as peerless.

The Category of the Ultimate describes in the most general way possible what it means to be a full reality, a complete or concrete moment of existence. The Ultimate Category expresses the ultimate dipolar contrast between a concrete whole and its parts. The Category is itself the least

---

3. Later, when discussing "entanglement," the possibility of an actual occasion simultaneously inheriting more than one superject will be examined.

concrete aspect of reality: It is the ultimate abstraction. The principle expressed by the Category is itself a common factor of all concrete facts, and, therefore, says nothing about how one fact does or could differ from another. Though each whole is necessarily unique, the principle that each concrete whole is unique is itself necessarily universal, the least unique aspect of reality. The most abstract characteristic of reality is necessarily true of every possible concrete thing.

Implicated in this category are the concepts of "whole," "one," "coming-to-be" or "process," "present," "*causa sui*" and their dipolar contrasts, "part," "many," "being," "past," "dependent," as well as "internal" and "external" relationships. A "whole" is a unit of process or coming-to-be bringing a new being into being. Process is a continuum of creative effort more fundamental, more inclusive, than being. It cannot be sufficiently explained as a function of one or more beings, though many beings are necessarily parts of a process. Created beings are the accomplishments of prior wholes that are immediately potencies for new wholes. Beings do, however, partially explain the new being that process is creating since, even though they do not add up to a sufficient condition, they are the necessary causes for the new being to be somewhat as it will be.

There is a basic ambiguity in the meaning of "becoming" only resolved with the articulation of the difference between epochal and modal principles: When the emphasis is on a whole becoming a part of another whole, "become" means the instantaneous transition from a self-empowered whole to a dependent reality as one ("privileged") ingredient in a new whole. When focusing on a whole becoming something new, "become" refers to the supreme or fragmentary mode of creative novelty exhibited by the moment during its temporal duration, during its life from its initiation to its termination. {Category of Explanation viii, "two descriptions are required for a actual entity: (a) one analytical of its potentiality for 'objectification' in the becoming of other actual entities, and (b) another which is analytical of the process which constitutes it own becoming." Category of Explanation xxii, "Thus 'becoming' is the transformation of incoherence into coherence . . ." (PR 25).} I would rather say it is a creative transformation from the loose generic coherence of the initial aim to a more specific embodiment.

The relation of being "in" is the dipolar relation of a part within the whole it partially determines or conditions. In the language of relations (which can be somewhat confusing because it is opposite the language of parts and wholes), when something A is externally related to another B, B can either be externally related to A (thus neither is a part of the other), or B can be internally related to A by having A as a part of itself (that is, A is a part of, and inside, B). When a part A is *in* the whole B, A is said to be "externally" related to B because nothing B does can change A.

There are two kinds of parts or aspects exhibited by all wholes:

(a) contingent parts: beings that have come to be, that is, beings created at some time that become the determinate parts of new process wholes, conditioning, in part, what those wholes can create and become, and

(b) necessary aspects: characteristics so fundamental they describe what it means to be any "whole" and are exhibited, therefore, as aspects of every possible whole.

Necessary "parts" or characteristics are the metaphysical principles themselves that *could never have been created* because they have always been exhibited as characteristics of all possible moments of creative process. A process, supposedly creating them, would have had to exhibit them during its supposed creating of them.

Every *successful* whole, at the end of its temporal extent, terminates in a determinate state which is the boundary between the process whole whose terminus it marks and a new whole that begins immediately with its prior's creation as its primary, "privileged" datum. All other beings that have come to be prior to, and contiguous to, the new whole, will also be initial data for the new actual entity. These created conditions are, therefore, partly descriptive of the spatially and temporally extended wholes in which they reside, but they are descriptions of contingent characteristics or causes, not of the unavoidable conditions that describe in part every possible whole.

Each whole is necessarily a spatial-temporal unit, a one, and each unit contains a multiplicity of others as parts, but these others are others as they have come to be and now are. Wholes cannot include other wholes as wholes: Wholes are processing units, and process cannot include another's process as a part of itself. Process wholes are subjects, and as Aristotle says, a subject cannot include, as part of itself, another subject. However, wholes can come to be, whereupon, contrary to Aristotle, they are no longer subjects but objects for new subjects.[4]

---

4. A possible qualification of the independence of process wholes, to be discussed later, may be what physicists call "entanglement." Here wholes may be linked during their creative efforts, not able to reach separate determinations until their entanglement "collapses."

The Categoreal Scheme

However, the necessity for a whole to simultaneously inherit many, a multiplicity of beings, requires reality to be a multiplicity of contemporary processes creating the beings that will be simultaneously inherited. The principle that "many become one," requires reality at all times to be an irreducible plurality of processing wholes. The necessity at every moment for reality to have many creating units that exist as mutual contemporaries is just as fundamental as the necessity for all beings that have come to be to exist as parts of new, successive wholes.

In Whitehead's statement that "The world is primordially many . . ." and "God is primordially one . . ." (*PR* 349), the oneness of God/dess is taken to reside both in the unique total inclusion of all accomplished processes in each divine process Whole and in the primordially and everlastingness of the divine personal society. "Primordial" will always be taken to mean that there was no first moment, just as "everlasting" will mean there can be no last moment. "Eternal" could be used to cover both if it were not so historically weighed down with the connotation of existing "out of time," a phrase likely having no meaning unless it means "in all moments of time." Whitehead may not have been clear on whether God/dess was one process or a primordial and everlasting series of actual entities, but serious logical problems arise trying to conceive of God/dess as one Whole, one actual entity that never begins nor ends. Further, his language at times seems to suggest that the divine primordial envisagement was a happening, a contingent, decisional grounding, not mythical shorthand for "always has been."

The fundamental necessity for reality to consist of a multiplicity of contemporaneous and successive "substances," is an emphatic denial that reality is one substance giving rise to many various modes, attributes or appearances as pantheisms and other substance philosophies maintain.

SECTION 2: PRINCIPLES OF EPOCHAL UNIVERSALITY— NECESSITIES EXHIBITED BY ALL WHOLES AT INITIATION AND THROUGHOUT THEIR CREATIVE PROCESSES

> The description of the generic character of an actual entity should include God, as well as the lowliest actual occasion . . . (*PR* 110).

Epochal categories are principles exhibited by all actual entities in the same way. They describe conditions essential for the formation of every

Process and Dipolar Reality

possible whole. Here it is true, as Whitehead says, that "the principles which actuality exemplifies all are on the same level" (*PR* 18). Both poles of each dipolar *epochal* category apply equally to all wholes, whereas the poles of the dipolar modal Categories distinguish some wholes from others, but do so on necessary, not contingent, grounds.

Each of the epochal principles makes more explicit one "same-level" aspect of the Ultimate Category that is implicit in all the others. The list of epochal Categories could be shortened or expanded, therefore, depending on one's purpose since these Categories are really synonyms of each other, each emphasizing and making explicit a certain aspect every fundamental unit of reality must exhibit, since "Each actual entity is analysable in an indefinite number of ways" (*PR* 19).

E1: Becomings include Beings--Creating includes Created—
Doing includes Done—Every being is either a completed process conditioning some successive wholes (that is, it is a contingently created part of some comings-to-be), or it is a necessary aspect of all possible contingent beings (that is, an aspect never created but has always been, (a) present as an unavoidable characteristic of all actual comings-to-be, (b) would have been present in any other actuality that could have come to be, and (c) will be present in every future coming to be).

> **E1a: Transition as Temporally Extensionless—**The transition from a process creating a being that is the terminus of the process to its "privileged" inclusion in a new process is immediate. The being created will also be inherited by other actual entities that begin somewhat after the actual entity that inherits the being as its privileged being. The being created is not a part in, nor felt by, the process that created it. {"No actual entity can be conscious of [feel] its own satisfaction;" (*PR* 85). Category of Explanation ii, "That in the becoming [transition or concrescence?] of an actual entity, the potential unity of many [creations] ... acquires the real unity of the one actual entity [the unity of one whole in process or one created determination?] ..." (*PR* 22).}
>
> **E1b: Being as Conditioning Process—**The being created as the result of each process of creating must be immediately part of the beginning of

another. {"*The Category of Conceptual Valuation*. From each physical feeling there is the derivation ["reproduction" (*PR* 26)] of a purely conceptual feeling whose datum is the eternal object determinant of the definiteness of the actual entity, or of the nexus, physically felt" (*PR* 26).} There is no "reproduction;" the inherited determination is just felt for what it is.

E1c: Process as Finite Temporal Extension—Every actuality must process; it must exhibit some temporal extension before ceasing, and cease it must. It terminates either (a) as a new being (datum) for others or (b) dies, failing to accomplish anything new.

Allowing some occasions to die before reaching new accomplishments seems to violate Whitehead's Categoreal Obligation, i, The Category of Subjective Unity: {"The many feelings which belong to an incomplete phase in the process . . . are compatible for integration by reason of the unity of their subject" (*PR* 26), and Category of Explanation xxii, "Thus 'becoming' is the transformation of incoherence into coherence, and in each particular instance ceases with this attainment" (*PR* 25).}

The reasoning for this major departure from Whitehead is discussed later, especially when the topic of the death of a person is examined. Though all actual entities cease, only two kinds must conclude with new determinate beings: (1) those forming the members of the cosmic Individual, and (2) those composing the members of the lowest-level society.

E2: Wholes include Parts—Every whole begins by including all beings prior and contiguous to its inception. {Category of Explanation iv: "every item in *its* universe [not *the* universe] is involved in each concrescence. . . . it belongs to the nature of a 'being' that it is a potential for every [successive and contiguous?] 'becoming'" (*PR* 22), emphasis added.}

E2a: Fully-Windowed Monads—Being is potency, and since potency is a continuum, every prior and contiguous being is fully included.

This principle of fully-windowed monads is, of course, contrary to Leibniz's windowless monads, but also may be contrary to Whitehead's peephole monads that apparently let some in and "negatively prehend" others or some of their parts. If by "negative prehension" Whitehead means that an actual entity's placement within the universe prohibits prehending those not contiguous to it at inception, then there is no disagreement. {"A negative prehension is the definite exclusion of the item from positive contribution to the subject's own real internal constitution" (*PR* 41). Category of Explanation xii: "two species of prehensions: (a) 'positive prehensions' ... termed 'feelings,' and 'negative prehensions' which are said to 'eliminate from feeling'" *PR* 23.}

E2b: Distinguishable but not Separable—Each created being is a complex of distinguishable, but not separable, parts. {Category of Explanation x: "the first analysis of an actual entity ... discloses it to be a concrescence of prehensions which ... originated ... its process of becoming" (*PR* 23). Category of Explanation xvii: "the many components of a complex datum have a unity: this unity is a 'contrast' of entities" (*PR* 24).} Contrasts, however, imply a whole that is more than the items contrasting, namely, that in, and by, which the contrasting items are simultaneously compared.

E2c: Each Process Whole Includes Many Beings as Determinate Parts—Every whole must begin by including many contiguous fragmentary beings and the most recent cosmically inclusive Being. Wholes are more than their parts but not apart from their parts.

E2d: One Part Common to All New Process Wholes—Every cosmic Whole includes one, and only one, *actualized* Whole that is both inclusive of all beings in existence as the Whole began and is contiguous to all new wholes. This is the latest cosmically inclusive Being and is the ground for the unity of cosmic reality and minimal cosmic order, despite the necessity for reality to be an irreducible multiplicity of processing actualities at all times.

E3: Subjects include Objects—Every object is a part of many successive subjects that contain it, including, always, the present cosmically inclusive Whole, and the fragmentary occasion that supersedes and inherits the "privileged" being. Every subject must contain many objects, directly and mediated.

E3a: Subjectivity—the Significance of the Present for Itself. An actuality, during its self-creating, feels others as having significance for itself in its goal to terminate as an object with significance for other subjects. {Category of Explanation xxiii, "An actual entity is called the 'subject' of is own immediacy" (*PR* 25). Categoreal Obligation vii, The Category of Subjective Harmony: "The valuations of conceptual feelings are mutually determined by the adaptation of those feelings to be contrasted elements congruent with the subjective aim" (*PR* 27).}

E3b: Temporally Finite Subjectivity—Every *successful* subject will cease existing as a subject and immediately be a "privileged" object in a new subject, a subject that will also include other objects. An unsuccessful subject ceases before creating a new being. {Category of Explanation xxv, "The final phase in the process of concrescence... is one complex, fully determinate feeling" (*PR* 25–26). The end of the final phase is not a feeling felt by the subject that created it because it (the superject) does not exist until the subject that created it has perished: "[N]o subject experiences twice... Actuality in perishing... loses subjective immediacy" (*PR* 29).}

E3c: Objective Identity—Each of the many object parts within a whole uniquely conditions the whole's subjectivity in one and only one way. Each inherited object can only be itself. It cannot function as if it were a multiplicity. This grounds the basis for self-consistency. {Category of Obligation ii, The Category of Objective Identity. "There can be no duplication of any element in the objective datum of the 'satisfaction' of an actual entity..." (*PR* 26). Category of Explanation xxvi, "Each element in the genetic process of an actual entity has one self-consistent function, however complex, in the final satisfaction" (*PR* 26).}

E3d: Objective Diversity—A multiplicity of objects cannot function as if they were only one. Spatial and qualitative contrasts cannot be ignored. Whitehead's Category of Transmutation, a *contingent* principle of organization (and, therefore, not truly a metaphysical principle), wherewith the details of the many are not retained, is not an exception to this principle since even with the loss of details, the result is different from the way it would be had there not been a multiplicity. Even when Transmutation does occur, the details are still in, and felt by, the actual entity. They simply are not felt with the awareness that the mode of Presentational Immediacy affords. {Category of Obligation iii, The Category of Objective Diversity. "There can be no 'coalescence' of diverse elements in the objective datum of an actual entity . . ." (*PR* 26).}

E4: Present includes Past—Accomplished feelings are parts of a present (subjective) feeling. {Category of Explanation xxiv, "The functioning of one actual entity in the self-creation of another actual entity is the 'objectification' of the former for the latter . . ." (*PR* 25).} Present (subjective) feeling must include past feelings (what others felt) as objective parts of its new subjective, present feeling.

    E4a: Past Accomplishments are Parts within present Comings-to-be.

    E4b: Distant past Accomplishments (inherited by the present occasion) are Parts within Parts . . . (and so on) of the Present.

E5: Present includes Future—The future is generic possibility (Epochal aspect) and possibility with different values (Modal aspect). {Category of Obligation viii, The Category of Subjective Intensity: "The subjective aim, whereby there is origination of conceptual feeling, is at intensity of feeling (α) in the immediate subject, and (β) in the *relevant* future . . . [namely,] those elements in the anticipated future which are felt with effective intensity by the present subject by reason of the real potentiality for them to be derived from itself" (*PR* 27).}

    E5a: Specific Aim—The immediate future for the present moment, is its *specific aim*, its "real potentiality." If one wants to distinguish the "specific aim" from the total potentiality found in the initial datum, one could say it is the most specific factor common to all simultaneously inherited beings. No whole can inherit the same objects as another and, therefore, the least generic aspect characterizing all the objects must be unique, thus every subjective aim is unique.

E5b: Objective Aim—Every moment's *ultimate aim* is a generic characteristic common to all possible moments: It is one of the ultimate generic aspects of each moment. The objective aim is the metaphysical aim, the necessary or most general context of all specific, contingent aims. It is called the "objective aim" since it is prior to any particular subject. It comes to all subjects as an aspect of every object felt, however vaguely. It is the only meaning that can be given to "pure potentiality."

E5c: Generic in Specific—The specific aim (the least generic aspect) includes all the more generic aims or potencies as aspects of each uniquely specified aim.

E5d: Partially Determinate Future—The future is already determined in part since whatever does occur must include what already is determinate in the present. {Category of Obligation ix, The Category of Freedom and Determination: "[I]n each concrescence whatever is determinable is determined . . . the decision of the whole arises out of the determination of the parts, so as to be strictly relevant to [them]" (*PR* 27–28).}

E5e: Partially Open Future—The future, as yet open to become determined, is not a set of specified possibilities (as Whitehead seems to speak of "eternal objects"). Potentiality is only specified insofar as specificity is brought into the present from the past. {Category of Obligation ix, The Category of Freedom and Determination: "The concrescence of each individual actual entity is internally determined and is externally free . . . beyond [present wholes] there is nonentity . . . [Concrescence] is the reaction of the unity of the whole to its own internal determination" (*PR* 27–28).}

E6: Specific Aim Includes What-Ought-to-Be—What is better to happen than not, is a range of possibility within the range of the specific aim (real potentiality) of the moment. {Category of Obligation viii, The Category of Subjective Intensity: "The subjective aim, whereby there is origination of conceptual feeling, is at intensity of feeling (α) in the immediate subject, and (β) in the *relevant* future . . . [namely,] those elements in the anticipated future which are felt with effective intensity by the present subject by reason of the real potentiality for them to be derived from itself" (*PR* 27).}

> **E6a: No One Best Possibility**—There is not "one best" (or "one worst"), nor even a set of specified bests, only a continuous range of possibility for each actual entity with specifics yet to be specified. The continuum contains possibilities to be specified of co-equal value at all levels.
>
> **E6b: Value Dimension of Possibilities**—What-ought-to-be in any particular circumstance is a range within what-might-be for that moment, given its circumstances. What does occur may be deficient in value relative to what could have been, depending on the modal status of the actual entity creating the value (see Model Category, M4).
>
> **E6c: Meaning of Value**—What "ought" to be in all possible circumstances must be. It is the unavoidable, metaphysical meaning of "value" namely, the completely generic aspect of all specific purposes. This metaphysical characteristic, also called the Objective or Ultimate Aim (*MT* 12), will be fulfilled in some way or other by every successful whole, and by each cosmic Whole in a way unsurpassed when it is created. "Is" and "ought" are identical at this level of complete abstraction and unsurpassed fulfillment.

E7: Evaluators include Evaluated—The evaluated is part of the evaluator. Every whole evaluates both its inherited physical facts and its new conceptual specifications in light of its specific goal's value range (which always includes the ultimate meaning of "value." See E5b). {Category of Obligation vii, The Category of Subjective Harmony: "The valuations of conceptual feelings are mutually determined by the adaptation of those feelings to be contrasted elements congruent with the subjective aim" (*PR* 27).}

E8: Order Includes Disorder—Disorder is always a part of a larger order that includes it and is partially disrupted by it.

E8a: Disorder Is Local—Disorder cannot be absolute. "Complete disorder" would be "complete novelty," which is meaningless. Disorder is always localized within a larger, more inclusive order it disrupts.

E8b: Inherited Disorder Establishes Aim—Every orderer (actual entity) requires some disorder, some *inherited* novelty (whether fortunate or not), to initiate its new creative ordering. Repeating just one past accomplishment *exactly* without any novelty is meaningless; only by inheriting many beings is the present presented with a novel situation which lays the basis for a new aim to be fulfilled (See E5a), since only by inheriting a unique *set* of past beings can one moment be distinguished from another. {Category of Explanation v, "no two actual entities originate from an identical universe" (*PR* 22).}

E8c: Tragedy and Evil's Possibility is Not Preventable—"Tragedy" is unfortunate and unchosen disorder that causes real possibility to be less fulfilling than would have been possible, perhaps even causing personal death before a new determinate accomplishment is achieved. "Evil" is the deliberate creating of disorder that causes future actual entities to be less enriched than they could have been without the specific disorder. Both arise from contingent causes, that is, any particular tragic or evil disruption could have been avoided had past decisions and circumstances been otherwise. Though the initiation of every moment requires some inherited novelty, the novelty created by tragedy and evil prevents other, more enriching possible novelties from occurring. "Insistence on birth at the wrong season is the trick of evil [and tragedy]" (*PR* 223). However, the *possibility* for tragic and evil happenings cannot be eliminated. Loss of future richness of experience is an unavoidable possibility because reality is populated by partially self-creating moments whose complete futures do not exist to be known and whose desires may be faulty by choice (evil) or ignorance (tragedy).

E9: Freedom includes Causation—Causation is a necessary condition for Freedom. {Category of Obligation ix, The Category of Freedom and Determination: "This final decision is the reaction of the unity of the whole to its own internal determination . . . [T]he decision of the whole arises out of the determination of the parts, so as to be strictly relevant to [them]" (*PR* 28).} The Category of Freedom and Determination is Whitehead's clearest statement of a dipolarly stated Category.

> **E9a: Environment Required**—Causation provides the environment, and so the opportunities, for the exercise of freedom.

> **E9b: Freedom is Finite, but Open**—The opportunity for freedom is provided by the inherited circumstances. Acting requires a goal, and a goal is only given as generic possibility embodied in an inherited, determinate datum. "Freedom," unless it is a response to what others' freedoms in the past has settled for the present, is meaningless. All potentiality is "real." "Pure potentiality" or "complete freedom" is meaningless. {Category of Explanation vi, "This indetermination, rendered determinate in the real concrescence, is the meaning of 'potentiality.' It is a conditioned indetermination, and is, therefore, called a 'real potentiality'" (*PR* 23).}

E10: Process' Novelty includes Permanence—Permanence is a conditioning of processes.

> **E10a: Lasting Permanence**—Stability over time (changelessness) arises because a characteristic persists from one moment to another. Societal permanence is either a function of an enduring personal nexus or of a non-personal society of such minimal complexity that every member inherits and passes on the same defining characteristic.

> **E10b: Everlastingness**—What is, but has not always been, was created by some moment. It survives as long as it is repeatedly inherited by new comings-to-be. There will always be some new actual entities or other

The Categoreal Scheme

or the reality of the past would be lost, a meaningless "possibility." (See Modal and Social categories for kinds of survival.)

E10c: Eternality—What has always been inherited (primordially), and will always be inherited (everlastingly), are eternal characteristics, namely, unavoidable metaphysical principles.

E11: Life includes the Dead—"Death," or perishing (as the satisfied determination of an actual occasion) is continually felt since it conditions new lives forever.

E11a: The "Death" (satisfaction) of a Moment is Included in the Inception of another Life Immediately Successive. The satisfied termination of an actual entity is never included in the actual entity that created it. New life is impossible without embracing accomplishments others' perishings provide.

E11b: The Death of a Person is the Failure of a Personal Society to Add a new Determination—The failure to reach a satisfaction is felt by other lives contiguous to where it would have occurred. "Death" of a personal series may be temporary for nondivine persons but is eventually permanent for all individuals but the one necessarily existing series, that is, the Individual whose momentary states are modally supreme (unsurpassed) when they occur; and when they are surpassed, they will only be surpassed by superseding moments of the Unsurpassable personal society itself. (See Modal and Social categories for kinds of survival.)

E12: Temporal Extension includes Spatial Extension—Spatiality is within temporality, that is, within a process.

E12a: Prehended Contemporaries—Processes, that are coming-to-be causally independent of each other and achieve their satisfactions prior and contiguous to a new whole that includes both their superjects, are mutually externally connected parts within that whole, exhibiting spatiality within that whole and within all future moments including that whole's satisfaction/superject as a part.

E12b: Temporality creates Space—Every temporally extended unit ceases, and if it ceases successfully creating a new result, it becomes one part of many parts that are related mutually externally to each other within one or more successive (temporally extended) actual entities, exhibiting spatial expansion.

E12c: Processing Contemporaries—Relations among contemporary *processing* wholes cannot be experienced until they are simultaneously objectified in superseding wholes extending over them. Objects related mutually externally are always within a process that is creating a new object containing them as determinate parts. These objects exhibit where and how the contemporaneous processes existed prior to their determinate objectifications.

E13: Extensive Quantity includes Quality—Qualities are spatio-temporally quantified, namely, this quality of feeling at this place (as opposed to other places) and during this process (as opposed to others). {Category of Explanation iii, "[I]n the becoming of an actual entity, novel prehensions, nexūs, subjective forms, propositions, multiplicities, and contrasts, also become" (*PR* 22).}

E13a: Specification—"Specification" is an extensive quantity qualified by feelings created during a moment's temporal extension's addition. {Category of Obligation v, The Category of Conceptual Reversion: "There is secondary origination of conceptual feelings with data which are partially identical with, and partially diverse from, the eternal objects [physically felt]" (*PR* 26). Category of Explanation vii, "The term 'ingression' refers to the particular mode in which the potentiality of an eternal object is realized in a particular actual entity, contributing to the definiteness of that actual entity" (*PR* 23). Category of Explanation xxiv, "The functioning of an eternal object in the self-creation of an actual entity is the 'ingression' of the eternal object in the actual entity" (*PR* 25).} Specification by "creation" is not the same as Whitehead's "ingression." Whitehead says "creating" is to be understood as the ingression into the present occasion of an object already specified eternally. The thesis here is that specifying occurs at the time of creation and is the very meaning of "creating."

E13b: Determination—"Determinateness" refers to a changeless quantified quality as an object in superseding subjective wholes that are conditioned by the determination. {Category of Explanation xx, "'Determination' is analysable into 'definiteness' and 'position,' where 'definiteness' is the illustration of select eternal objects, and 'position' is relative status in a nexus of actual entities" (*PR* 25).}

SECTION 3: PRINCIPLES OF DIPOLAR MODAL CONTRASTS—CATEGORIES CONTRASTING CONDITIONAL AND UNCONDITIONAL WHOLES AT BIRTH AND DURING GROWTH

There is the vague sense of many which are one; and of one which includes the many ... there are two senses of the one—namely, the sense of the one which is all, and the sense of the one among the many (*MT* 110).

The presumption that there is only one genus of actual entities constitutes an ideal of cosmological theory to which the philosophy of organism endeavours to conform. The description of the generic character of an actual entity should include God, as well as the lowliest actual occasion, though there is a specific difference between the nature of God and that of any occasion (*PR* 110).

At least two basic forms of contrast are not abolished by metaphysical conceptions. One is that between God and any other individual being; the other is that between logical types ... [A] metaphysician must eschew extreme nominalism [and] admit that distinctions of logical type have counterparts in extra-linguistic reality ... Metaphysics by definition takes necessity to be ontological as well as logical ... In addition to the most general or neutral idea of reality, spanning all logical types, we need metaphysical universals valid only within one type ... For where there are no definite common aspects there are no definite contrasts either (*CSPM* 138–142).

Though the principles of epochal dipolarity are common to all actual entities, still the quantity of their inclusiveness and the quality of their creative processes differ. Most differences amongst occasions are factual or contingent differences reflecting the different standpoint and creative ability each has.

So even though it is true that many "principles which actuality exemplifies all are on the same level," still actual entities "differ among themselves ... [by] gradations of importance, and diversities of function ..." (*PR* 18). But Whitehead also says there is a "specific difference between the nature of God and that of any occasion" (*PR* 110).

I submit that insofar as Whitehead's characterization of God is taken to be one actual entity rather than one personal society, God's difference from other actual occasions is greater than a "specific difference" since all actual entities can only create one thing, can only come to be once. God, conceived as one persistent subject, would be the only reality that could act out of self-interest, since no other actual entity can inherit its own creation.

Some differences among actual entities, however, are not contingent differences; some are necessary, modal differences. Modality is the principle more clearly articulated by Hartshorne than Whitehead that actual entities not only happen to differ among themselves in contingent ways, but that some differ from others *necessarily*.

So using Whitehead's term, there are two "species" of actual entities: those that happen to differ from each other, and those that must differ from each other. Since all actual entities create outcomes that are partly the result of contingent choices, a more accurate characterization of the two species would be: Some actual entities, those that are supreme or unsurpassed, differ from others in *some* necessary ways, and some actual entities, those that are not supreme, differ from others only in contingent ways.

When it comes to *how* actual entities exist, all exist contingently, since none must exist just as it does, but perhaps it makes sense that one "personal" society of actual entities exists unsurpassably which would require it to exist necessarily or be surpassable by one that did. Just because every actual entity exists contingently does not even preclude a non-personal *society* existing necessarily: A society composed of non-supreme members would exist necessarily if it were required to always have some contingent members or other.

Concern for the metaphysical characteristics of societies in addition to the characteristics of individual actual entities sets the metaphysical

The Categoreal Scheme

discussion in the widest possible context, the context that discusses the Categories of societal organization and the contrasts actual entities necessarily and contingently exhibit.

The Modal Principles further specify the Ultimate and Epochal Categories by distinguishing actual entities that are necessarily supreme in the manner of their existence from those that are not. Here again is another dipolarity, namely, the contrast *within* those actualities that are supremely Whole between those that are supreme and those that are not.

To call an actual occasion a "fragment" of reality, that is, one that is not supreme in its inclusiveness, requires knowing what a "Whole," non-fragmental, actual entity means in order to know what a "fragment" means. To be a supreme Whole implies a Whole inclusive of all those that are not supremely whole because to unquestionably surpass another implies the surpasser must include those surpassed as parts of itself. To be "parts" implies a whole in which they are parts; to be parts of all there is implies a Whole that includes all there is. Likewise, a qualitative dimension deficient in quality implies a quality that is not deficient or there would be no standard to weigh the value of qualities that fall short.

Subsection 1: Modal Categories of Quantity and Perspective—Saving Value at Transition

> Category of Explanation xi . . . every prehension consists of three factors: (a) the "subject" . . . (b) the "datum" . . . [and] (c) the "subjective form" . . . (*PR* 23).

Transitions from the multiplicity of determinate accomplishments to new creative efforts at each moment consist of one supreme Whole and many fragmentary wholes. They are a true multiplicity wherein all are in causal independence from each other. Prior accomplishments being mediated by the members of the multiplicity are no longer members of the immediate multiplicity.

M1: At every Moment one Supreme, Non-perspectival Whole includes all Satisfied Perspectival Wholes—At each moment there must be one, and only one Whole, that includes and saves all beings created up to the inception of that moment. {Category of Explanation v: "[N]o two actual entities originate from an identical universe" (PR

22)}, that is, from the same multiplicity of others' determinate creations, and only one can be all-inclusive.

M1a: Spatial All-Inclusiveness—Every fragmentary whole's accomplishment is a part of the next all-inclusive Whole. All space (that is, all those fragmentary accomplishments that are mutually externally related) is contained in the next cosmic Whole. Cosmic Wholes cannot take a perspective on the accomplishment of any whole since a perspective requires partial inclusion and partial exclusion of the multiplicity of beings. {Category of Explanation xiv: "[A] nexus is a set of actual entities . . . constituted by their prehensions of each other . . . [that is, prehensions of past members by present members] . . ." (PR 24).} There can be one, and only one, personal nexus that is cosmically inclusive at each moment.

M1b: Spatial Expansiveness—Each new cosmically inclusive Whole is spatially richer than previous Wholes in the cosmic personal nexus because it contains, (1) all the new fragmentary creations with their mutually external connectedness that immediately prior occasions created, and (2) all earlier creations now being mediated by these most recent occasions, as well as (3) all the innumerable prior and mediated satisfactions of the cosmically inclusive personal series itself.

M1c: Temporal Omniscience—The temporal extent of each cosmically all-inclusive moment is at least as short as any other, ensuring nothing any perspectival (fragmentary) moment creates is lost between divine moments.

M1d: Spatial-Temporal Omnipresence and Causal Ubiquity—The most recent supreme Whole's accomplishment is contiguous to every new whole, so every whole must include the most recent all-inclusive Whole's creation. Each supreme Whole and each fragmentary whole must include all of the latest supreme superject, though most of the cosmic past is insignificant for perspectival wholes because it is not reinforced by the actualizations of prior and contiguous non-supreme wholes. {"The 'superjective nature' of God is the character of the pragmatic value of his specific satisfaction qualifying the transcendent creativity in the various temporal [non-divine] instances" (PR 88)},

The Categoreal Scheme

though some will argue that Whitehead believes there is only one divine satisfaction.

M2: Each Moment there must be Many Contemporaneous Perspectival Wholes.

M2a: Perspectival Inclusions—Every fragmentary whole must start with, (1) the most recent all-inclusive Whole's created determination, and (2) all the determinations created by fragmentary wholes prior and contiguous to its initiation. {Category of Explanation xiv, "[A] nexus is a set of actual entities . . . constituted by their prehensions of each other [that is, prehensions of past members by present members] . . ." (PR 24).}

M2b: Unique Selection of Perspectival Exclusions—Every fragmentary whole will exclude at its inception some actualizations others will include, namely, those not contiguous to it. The beings contiguous to the foundation of a new fragmentary whole are a unique set: No other whole will include and exclude the same set of beings. {Category of Explanation v, "[N]o two actual entities originate from an identical universe" (PR 22).}

M2c: Multiple Fragmentary Creations—For the founding of each moment, many beings created by prior and contiguous wholes are required, because all wholes (including supreme Wholes) require more than one previous determination as their causal data, since every actual entity must inherit a non-personal nexus to set up its spatiality and to provide the novelty required to establish its aim. (See also, E2c: Wholes include Parts).

Subsection 2: Modal Categories of Quality and Growth—Creating Value during Process

Category of Explanation xviii, the Ontological Principle: All explanation resides "*either* in the character of some actual[ized] entity [or entities] in the actual[ized] world of that concrescence, *or* in the character of the subject which is in process of concrescence" (*PR* 24 and 43).

The multiplicity of contemporaneous creative efforts in process together consists of one supreme Whole and many fragmentary wholes. Reality at each moment is an irreducible multiplicity of actual entities in process.

M3: Each Supreme Whole's Creative Effort is Unsurpassed in Value— Each unconditional Whole uses its moment of life to create a result as enriching as any other possible given the parts it must include, namely, all the beings, all the specified determinations, created up to that moment by all prior cosmic Wholes and all fragmentary wholes. The next unconditional Whole must also include the Being just created which is its immediately prior Whole's creation, its "privileged" datum, and so on *ad infinitum* into the past since there is no first actual entity.

M3a: Every Supreme Whole begins Immediately upon Completion of the Prior Whole in the Unsurpassable Personal Nexus— Even though every supreme dipolar actual entity begins with prior determinations and ends with a newly specified determination, creative process is continuous from one actual entity to the next: Cosmic process never began, nor can it ever end. Each supreme satisfaction is only possible as a "privileged" datum for the next Whole, which also prehends all beings initiating all fragmentary occasions since each is contiguous to the initiation of the new cosmic Whole.

M3b: Indistinctness within Clarity— Each Supreme Whole includes all others with complete clarity, including clearly knowing the precise vagueness and indistinctness by which fragmentary wholes feel others.

M3c: Unsurpassed Value— The meaning of unsurpassed "beauty," "love," "goodness" and "clarity," (as with all value terms *that can be conceived supremely*) is exhibited in the actualizing and actualization of every non-fragmentary Whole. Concrete fulfillments of these value abstractions are metaphysically necessary in some way or other, and always by the present Whole in a way no other whole can equal or surpass.

M4: Some Fragmentary Wholes or Other Must Create Qualified Value—Though no particular fragmentary wholes are necessary, some fragmentary wholes or other are necessary. There must be ever on-going creations of new conditional values. The value of every satisfied conditional whole is immediately a "privileged" datum in a new conditional whole, along with all other beings contiguous to its inception, including the latest unconditional Creation.

M4a: Unavoidable Perspective—Every conditional whole's value will fall short of the unsurpassed Whole's value because fragmentary wholes cannot create a result inclusive of all others' accomplishments. {Category of Explanation xii, "[N]egative prehensions'... are said to 'eliminate from feeling'... A negative prehension holds its datum as inoperative in the progressive concrescence of prehensions constituting the unity of the subject" (*PR* 23).} The view maintained here is that only non-contiguous beings are "negatively" prehended, that is, simply left out.

M4b: Surpassed Clarity—Every conditional whole's value will fall short of the unsurpassed Whole's value not only because it cannot include all the beings in existence, but also because it cannot contain and retain all that it does include with complete clarity (compare Leibniz's confused monads). {Categoreal Obligation vi, the Category of Transmutation: "[I]n a subsequent phase of integration of these simple physical feelings together with the derivate conceptual feeling, the prehending subject may transmute the *datum* of this conceptual feeling into a characteristic of some *nexus* ..." (*PR* 27).} Transmutation is not necessary and so is not a metaphysical Category.

M4c: Temporal Duration—The epochal duration of fragmentary occasions must endure longer than the temporal extent of supreme Wholes to ensure everything created will be saved as part of the ever-expanding, all-inclusive determinate past.

M4d: Privileged Part—Every *successful* actual occasion is the "privileged" part in the next occasion of the personal nexus. All other beings contiguous to the initiation of the new whole were created just prior to the privileged being and are sustained by other processes.

Process and Dipolar Reality

> **M4e: Fragmentary Occasion's Failure**—Any particular fragmentary occasion, after struggling for at least as long as a divine's durational epoch, may fail to bring a new determination into being, that is, it may die, being overwhelmed with unintegrable diversity. {This principle violates Whitehead's Categoreal Obligation, i, The Category of Subjective Unity: "The many feelings which belong to an incomplete phase in the process . . . are compatible for integration by reason of the unity of their subject" (*PR* 26).}

Since the subjective aim is simply another way to refer to the unique feeling of all the elements of the inherited datum felt simultaneously as the ground for new specification and determination, what is at stake here is the ability of the actual entity to bring about a new, more specific determination within the scope of the somewhat generic potentiality provided by the aim. At the initiation of the occasion the aim is more general than it is just before the moment's newly created specifications. If the inherited data are so disorganized relative to the inheriting actual occasion that the limited creative ability of the occasion cannot keep them in sufficient harmony (as the occasion processes from a general goal to a more definite goal), the moment may give up and die without any new accomplishment. Whitehead's position on this (that all actual entities that begin must conclude by creating a new being) makes very problematic understanding how the death of a personal series is possible.

> **M4f: The Death of a Personal Society**—The death of a personal series of moments is the failure of the last moment of the series to create a new determination. For personal societies, other than the Unsurpassable's and those forming the personal strands of the least complex, non-personal society, it may be possible to have a hiatus in the series, a temporary death, whereby a new whole does not follow immediately, but does eventually occur.

SECTION 4: ENTITY TYPES AND PRINCIPLES OF SOCIAL ORGANIZATION—CATEGORIES OF NECESSARY CONTRASTS WITHIN PROCESS WHOLES

> [B]elief in a final order, popular in religious and philosophic thought, seems to be due to the prevalent fallacy that all types of

The Categoreal Scheme

seriality necessarily involve terminal [and initial?] instances (*PR* 111).

Most organizational relationships are contrasts that have been created: They are contingent aspects of cosmological order. However, there are some principles of organization that are metaphysical, required for any possible, created cosmological order.

Maintaining the difference between a "multiplicity," a "whole," and an "individual" or "person" is essential in clarifying these contrasts. A "whole" is the most fundamental unit of creative process, an actual entity. An "individual" or "person" is a series of wholes, such that each whole of the serial nexus becomes a *privileged* part of the next whole, and the most recent whole of the series contains the prior members of the series as determinate parts. Of the following Categories, only the first two, S1 and S2a, concern full actualities, that is, processing wholes. The others describe subordinate aspects or parts found in wholes.

S1: Actual Entities—Actual entities, also called "actual occasions" (nondivine moments only), "full actualities," "wholes," "subjects," "moments of creativity," "units of process," "*causa sui*."

These are the only fully real entities. Nothing exists in addition to these units. Each fundamental reality is a dipolar contrast between its inherited determinate parts, its physical causes, and the creating mentality of the whole that contains them and partly (largely) consists of them. Even though every whole is contingent in the particular way it comes to be during its creative effort, each exhibits all the Epochal necessities and its side of the Modal necessities. {Category of Existence i, "Actual Entities (also termed Actual Occasions), *or* final Realities, or *Res Verae*." Category of Existence vi, Propositions, *or* Matter of Fact in Potential Determination, *or* Impure Potentials for the Specific Determination of Matters of Fact, *or* Theories" (*PR* 22). Category of Explanation xix, "the fundamental types of entities are actual entities, and eternal objects" . . . Category of Explanation xxi, "An entity is actual, when it has significance for itself . . . Thus an actual entity combines self-identity with self-diversity." Category of Explanation xxii, "an actual entity . . . plays diverse roles in self-formation without losing its self-identity" (*PR* 25).} An actual entity is a proposition, a lure for new feeling. Its subject is the inherited data and its predicate is the subjective aim, the datum felt subjectively.

S2: Multiplicities—A "multiplicity" is either (a) many actual*izing* entities in process together, not influencing each other, or (b) many actual*ized* entities as objectified in an actual entity and considered in abstraction from the whole including them. {Category of Explanation xvi: "[A] multiplicity consists of many entities, and its unity is constituted by the fact that all its constituent entities severally satisfy at least one condition which no other entity satisfies" (*PR* 24).}

> **S2a: Process Multiplicities**--Reality is an irreducible multiplicity of process wholes. There are always many actual entities in process together though not necessarily beginning or ending together. Each of the many includes one non-fragmentary Whole and many fragmentary wholes, contemporaneously in process. As actualities in process, even each supreme Whole is "one among the many" (*MT* 110).

The members of the multiplicity of processes are not parts of a whole including them and comparing them. While "in process" they cannot be contrasted with each other. No process unit, which is a subject experiencing, can be an object for another's experience. However, the determinate parts inherited by a processing whole, say M, are accessible to other nascent actual entities, say N and O, to be parts of their initial causal datum (even before M reaches its own determinate satisfaction), if those nascent subjects are contiguous to the determinate parts (beings) contained in M even though M is still coming-to-be.

That reality is such a fundamental plurality is a conjecture justified by their creations which are objects for another's experience, an experience that does exhibit the coordinate relationships the members of the actualizing multiplicity had as subjects and now have with each other as objects within the inclusive, actualizing entity. These objectified contrasts are only possible because each member of the contrasting multiplicity (as felt within and by a whole) was created by a prior processing subject.

The Categoreal Scheme

All contrasts are characteristics within wholes. Only wholes are able to grasp many simultaneously and compare their differences. Reality's multiplicity of processes cannot be reduced to aspects of one underlying unity except in the sense that they all have at least one identical part (the previous cosmic Whole's creation), and they will all become parts in the next cosmically inclusive Whole. Pantheism is not the ultimate structure of reality. Every new contrast of externally related others is a force towards qualitative enrichment and quantitative expansion. {Category of Existence vii, Multiplicities or Pure Disjunctions of Diverse Entities. Category of Explanation i: "[T]he actual world is . . . process, and . . . process is the becoming of actual entities" (*PR* 22). "Thus the ultimate metaphysical truth is atomism" *PR* 35.}

> **S2b: Prehended Multiplicities**—The diverse beings embraced as parts of a new actuality as it begins can be considered a multiplicity in abstraction from the whole that contains them. Many immediately prior and contiguous actualizations are required, one of which must be the last cosmic creation since its created determination (object/superject/Being) is contiguous to all new moments as they begin. {Category of Explanation xvi: "[A] multiplicity consists of many entities, and its unity is constituted by the fact that all its constituent entities severally satisfy at least one condition which no other entity satisfies" (*PR* 24).} In this case, they are, at least, all parts in the same whole.

S3: "Eternal" Objects—The only *eternal* objects are the metaphysical principles themselves: necessary characteristics of all possible wholes. They are "complete abstractions," never-created objects. In this sense there is agreement with Whitehead that "there are no novel eternal objects" (*PR* 22, Category of Explanation iii). This Category, S3, is a severe limitation on Whitehead's definition of "eternal objects." {Category of Existence v: "Eternal Objects or Pure Potentials for the Specific Determination of Fact, or Forms of Definiteness" (*PR* 22).}

S4: Created, Conceptual Objects (as a class)—No *particular* created, that is, specified, conceptual object is necessary; only some

31

conceptual objects or other are necessary in the self-development of an actual entity. Only the class of created, conceptual objects is necessarily not empty. Process reality, that is, the subjective process of creating, necessarily makes contingent specifications, which, if made determinate in a satisfaction, become changeless objects for future others. Each supreme Whole will always succeed in establishing a new determinate satisfaction as a "privileged" datum in the next Whole; only some fragmentary wholes or other must be successful, namely, those in the lowest-level society. {Category of Obligation v: "Conceptual Reversion: There is secondary origination of conceptual feelings..." (*PR* 26). Category of Existence iv: "Subjective Forms, or Private Matters of Fact" (*PR* 22).}

S4a: **Conceptual Objects as non-Determinate Specifications**—Objects created by the whole for itself. Conceptual specifications of potentiality made during processes before they reach a determinate result. {Categoreal Obligation v, Conceptual Reversion: "There is secondary origination of conceptual feelings..." (*PR* 26).}

S4b: **Conceptual Objects Contrasting with Inherited Objects**—The conceptual whole (or a conceptual aspect of it) contrasting with inherited, "physical" objects. {Categoreal Obligation v, The Category of Conceptual Reversion: "There is secondary origination of conceptual feelings..." (*PR* 26)}, namely, feelings in addition to those of the initial datum.

S4c: **Conceptual Objects Contrasting with Conceptual Objects**— The contrast of two or more conceptual objects originated during an actuality's growth.

S4d: **Conceptual Objects as Determinate Specifications**—Objects specified during a whole's process that become fixed or determinate aspects of the whole's satisfied termination. A conceptual creation that survives to become determinate or actual*ized*, does not exist as determinate in the actual entity that created it. It is immediately a part and a cause in another, another that is "privileged" to be the primary recipient of its predecessor's creation. {Category of Explanation xxv:

The Categoreal Scheme

"The final phase in the process of concrescence . . . is one complex, fully determinate feeling. This final phase is termed the 'satisfaction'" (*PR* 25).}

S5: Created and Determinate (Physical) Objects (as a class)—No *particular* determination is necessary, only some one or other is necessary for all successful actual entities. Both the class of satisfied fragmentary actualities and the class of supreme Wholes is necessarily not empty. Neither class has had a first member nor will it have a last member. Each determinate satisfaction will be a cause, a physical object for others. {Category of Existence ii: "Prehensions or Concrete Facts of Relatedness." Category of Existence iii: "Nexūs, or Public Matters of Fact" (*PR* 22).} Conceptual feelings are fluid along continua; physical feelings are internally unalterable, however, their significance is adjustable relative to others in the whole.

S5a: Spatial Multiplicities or Simultaneous, Coordinate Contrasts—Contemporaneous contrasts: Objective multiplicities of mutually externally connected determinations, that is, the direct inheritances of many others' creations. Only one Whole at each moment can and must inherit *all* new creations. Some others at each moment can and must inherit only some (less than all) of the new creations: These are "fragmentary" wholes. {Category of Explanation xx: "''Determination' is analysable into 'definiteness' and 'position'. . ." (*PR* 25).}

S5b: Temporal Multiplicities or Successive Contrasts—Mediated multiplicities. Every actual entity inherits actual*ized* others embedded in those it directly inherits as parts, that is, as mediated by those that are prior and contiguous to itself that it immediately inherits. The primordial past is presented to the present as mediated, as a part of each present's immediate parts, *ad infinitum* from the past.

S6: Individuals as Persons—A strict "individual," or "person," is a series of wholes wherein each successor inherits each *privileged* predecessor's accomplishment in the series plus contiguous others, since there is no individual that inherits just its own past. Every moment of every individual must also inherit what some others just accomplished. {Category of Explanation xiv: "[A] nexus is a set of actual entities ... constituted by their prehensions of each other ..." (*PR* 24).} Whitehead here is a bit careless or cryptic: There can be no prehension of actual entities in process and no mutual prehension of just actual*ized* entities: If A includes B, B cannot include A.

S6a: Necessary Individual—Only the Individual who is tolerant of any conceivable environment can exist necessarily. This one Individual, only, could never have had a first moment and must have new moments forever. This Individual is the primordial and everlasting One, the sense in which the temporal universe is one. This Individual is the temporally all-inclusive One as well as the spatially all-inclusive One, the one that includes all contrasts that exist at each temporal moment. Together, both temporal and spatial all-inclusiveness, express "the sense of the one which is all" (*MT* 110). However, this all-inclusiveness cannot include the many fragmentary others that are in process contemporaneously with the present all-inclusive Actual Entity: the sense in which the Whole is "one among the many" (*MT* 110).

S6b: Contingent Individuals—All contingent individuals (except those of the lowest-level personal strands) have a first moment and have had, or will have, a last moment. Not only is every moment not necessary as it is, as is the case for all moments, but it is not necessary that any fragmentary personal series exists at all that is more complex than the strands of the lowest-level society: That reality forms complex personal strands in addition to the unsurpassable nexus, is not necessary. A minimally enriching world would not perpetuate complex personal order if every contingent past part inherited by each perspectival moment were equally important. There would be no focus resulting from past fortunate order, that is, spontaneous differences would not stand out to be repeated or enlarged upon by present decisions or inherited circumstances. That the world is not so tedious, testifies to the creative urge to enrich experience through the creation of complex personal societies.

S7: Contrasts of Contrasts—Accumulated contrasts. Every moment inherits others' accomplishments that contrast with each other within that moment's whole. These contrasts will then contrast with newly created conceptualizations in the present whole and with other, determinate contrasts in successive wholes. The affect of these contrasts may be trivial or significant. The dipolar modal necessities only require that one Individual inherit all contrasts, and that there be some minimal perspectival experiences or other inheriting some contrasts. The varieties and effects of higher contrasts are contingent creations. The many forms of contrast are strategies used by fragmentary wholes to create more enriched feelings, given their unavoidable perspective and limited creative ability. These strategies give to cosmically clear experience what unsurpassable experience with its complete clarity cannot have on its own, namely, the experience of confusion. In this sense God/dess evolves as nature evolves. {Category of Existence viii: "Contrasts, or Modes of Synthesis of Entities in one Prehension, or Patterned Entities" (*PR* 22). Category of Explanation xvii: "[T]he many components of a complex datum have a unity: this unity is a 'contrast' of entities" (*PR* 24).} This "unity" of contrast can only exist, however, within the process of an actualizing entity, a process whole; to think otherwise is to commit the Fallacy of Misplaced Concreteness.

Chapter 3

Metaphysics and Change
Principles of Epochal Universality

> The most general sense of the meaning of change is "the differences between actual occasions in one event" (*PR* 80).

WHITEHEAD'S INSIGHT THAT SOMETHING changing is really a series of creative of processes, each of which does not change, but comes to be and remains what it is forever, is certainly a major contribution to metaphysics. The historical attempts to explain change all have serious logical problems, failing in one way or other to make sense of how something can alter and still be the same thing that altered. Parmenides was right that change cannot be meaningfully rationalized so long as what is actual*ized*, what is in being, is given primary status: The basic units of wholeness cannot be units of being. But Whitehead did not just deny the primacy of being by championing becoming over being; Heraclitus had attempted this millennia before, at least for the realm of sense experience. Whitehead said that dipolarity is the key: "Any instance of experience is dipolar, whether that instance be God or an actual occasion of the world" (*PR* 36).

However, given a dipolarity in which being is the primary or inclusive term and process or coming-to-be is a part of that being, the whole (being) alters so the whole is not the same whole it is/was, the contradiction Parmenides pointed out. But given a dipolarity in which process or coming-to-be is the inclusive term, one can agree with Parmenides that

Metaphysics and Change

being is changeless: Once a being has come to be, it must remain what it is as a changeless part of new units of coming-to-be.

"Change" then makes sense as the comparison or contrast of what came to be to what comes to be later, in the "same thing," that is, the same "personal" series. Beings, contrary to Parmenides and many since, are not just things that always are and have always been; they are created; they come to be. They come to be at some place and time in the complex cosmic extensive spatial-temporal nexus and forever after require other creative comings-to-be to be partly as they are because they came to be just as they did where they did. As they come to be, they are "ob-jects" "thrown towards," "cast in front of" those that come after, providing them with stumbling blocks or stepping stones.

Still, the ancient world's belief that beings cannot come into being is so seductive that even Whitehead defines "creativity" as "ingression" of *eternal* beings into the units of process from an eternal realm, emphasizing that "there are no novel eternal objects" (*PR* 22), essentially Plato's attempted answer to Parmenides. "Eternal objects," at least those that are not descriptive of the truly never-created metaphysical dimensions of reality, must be created; they must come to be.

Yet, an epochally grounded metaphysics raises other issues, for example, how to understand the temporal solidarity of the universe if wholes don't survive more than one moment. The quick, short answer to this issue is that a personal series, or as Whitehead says, a "personal nexus," maintains a strong temporal unity because the present builds around the changeless and (everlastingly) persistent past. The past is literally part of the present: The past is present *in* the present. In dipolar categories, every determinate being can only be a subordinate part. The past is settled and partial; the present is a whole working towards a settlement, and in so doing, carries within itself all the past's contiguous prior deeds.

Still there are questions of origin: How do new moments start? Why do they extend over, or inherit, just those of the past it does? How does a personally ordered, societal nexus become established? Can a process once initiated fail to create a new being? If not, how and why would a personal series die? Is there, must there be, a non-perspectival, cosmically inclusive series? If so, how does such a modally supreme personal series of moments relate to occasions that are modally deficient? Is a non-divine, society of perspectival occasions necessary?

The universe is populated with dipolar actual entities, each of which must display all the characteristics or Categories common to all actual entities as well as contingent characteristics that are unique to each actual occurrence. Metaphysics seeks to find the conditions that are discoverable by conceptual analysis alone, namely, those conditions that define what it means to exist as such, not what it means to exist as this as opposed to that. That "every actual entity is unique" is an absolutely non-unique (metaphysical) factor of every actual entity. However, since reality is necessarily dipolar, there will be differences of kind between actual entities. When actual entities necessarily differ from each other, how they differ can be discoverable by conceptual analysis alone given adequate insight.

The necessary differences actual entities exhibit are modal differences, that is, differences between actual entities that must fulfill the Categories supremely and those that can't. A proposal for a metaphysical scheme that does not examine the possibility that this modal distinction is meaningful, fails to consider all the logical possibilities. Even if every actual entity is contingent in how it comes to be, still one must allow that some actual entities can or must be as inclusive as possible, that is, simply all-inclusive, or as Hartshorne says, "non-fragmentary," and others must not be all-inclusive, that is, they must be "fragmentary."

All of what is actually included in an all-inclusive actual entity may be unknowable (at least to us), but we can know (if metaphysics is a rational undertaking) what it means to be "all-inclusive" or not, without knowing any created or contingent details about what is included and how it exists. Being "all-inclusive" is just one of many concepts that must be considered when modally superior actual entities are defined and when the "modally unsurpassable personal society of supreme actual entities" is defined. But before taking up the modal differences actual entities must exhibit, a couple points on the epochal characteristics all actual entities must exhibit "in the same way."

Every actual entity begins with, (a) feelings of others' accomplishments, (b) an urge to do something different from those others, and (c) a direction or vector the urge to novelty will or should take. In Whitehead's terminology, data, creativity, and subjective aim.

An actual entity is one epoch, that begins by feeling the determinate conditioning of others' accomplishments; seeks in its finite life-span to accomplish something for future actual entities; and ceases when its seeking is satisfied or its creative energy is insufficient to create a new determination because its initial conditioning was too chaotic. Whitehead does not seem to consider the possibility an occasion can fail to accomplish something new once it is established (see Categoreal Obligation i, The Category of Subjective Unity, *PR* 26), but Whitehead fails to consider a possible Modal dimension: necessary fulfillment versus merely possible or contingent fulfillment. Requiring every actual entity to reach a determinate satisfaction makes understanding the Category of the Ultimate and the death of a personal nexus problematic.

Chapter 4

Basic Anatomy of an Actual Entity
Discussion of the Dipolar Epochal Categories

> According to this account, the experience of the simplest grade of actual entity is to be conceived as the unoriginative response to the datum with its simple content of sensa (*PR* 115).

ACTUAL ENTITIES COME IN all degrees of complexity, though most of their complexity does not arise from metaphysical necessity, but is due rather to contingent enhancements, namely, decisions and accidents. An examination of the conditions for minimally creative occasions should reveal just those conditions every actual entity must exhibit. Yet, even restricting this examination to metaphysical conditions requires one to focus on more than one actual occasion since all actual and actualized entities exist as members of social groups. Every actual entity begins with what others have created and gives to others what it creates. Also, each is always one of many simultaneously in process as contemporaries.

Even so, it is usual to begin an analysis of the anatomy of an actual entity with the "basic situation," that is, the transition from others to the new subject. Here we are immediately confronted with one of the most controversial aspects of Whitehead's system: Where does the creativity of the new whole, the inclusive pole of the dipolar entity, come from since the included pole, the inheritances from others, by themselves are passive? Consider the following passage from *Adventures of Ideas* written after

Basic Anatomy of an Actual Entity

Process and Reality. Here Whitehead is revisiting this concern that *Process and Reality* didn't adequately address.

> The initial situation includes a factor of activity, which is the reason for the origin of that occasion of experience. This factor of activity is what I have called "Creativity." The initial situation with its creativity can be termed the initial phase of the new occasion. It can equally well be termed the "actual world" relative to that occasion. It has a certain unity of its own, expressive of its capacity of providing the objects requisite for a new occasion, and also expressive of its conjoint activity whereby it is essentially the primary phase of a new occasion. It can thus be termed a "real potentiality." The "potentiality" refers to the passive capacity; the term "real" refers to the creative activity, where the Platonic definition of "real" in the Sophist is referred to. This basic situation, this actual world, this primary phase, this real potentiality—however you characterize it—as a *whole* is active with its inherent creativity, but in its details it provides the passive objects which derive their activity [effectiveness] from the creativity of the whole. The creativity is the actualization of potentiality, and the process of actualization is an occasion of experiencing. Thus viewed in abstraction objects are passive, but viewed in conjunction they carry the creativity which drives the world. The process of creation is the form of unity of the Universe (*AI* 179, emphasis added).

In any description of the life cycle of an actual entity, its dipolar structure must be kept foremost in mind. The subordinate side of the dipolarity is, in Whitehead's words, the "basic situation," the "actual[ized] world," the "primary phase," the "real potentiality" of the actual entity. They are "passive objects." The creative process itself is the dipolar *whole*[5] that includes the objects as "details" or parts. These parts "carry" the creative energy of the whole which is actualizing the potentiality provided by the "actual world." Dipolarity is not correctly characterized as a whole *and* parts. The whole is partly its parts, and when the actual entity begins, the whole is nearly only its parts. The only aspect of the incipient whole not found in the parts and their given coordinate arrangement, is the simultaneity of feeling of all the parts. The parts are not felt serially, one after another, but all at once. Whitehead often expresses this by using the singular to refer to the

---

5. I cannot emphasize enough that a "whole" is the spatially and temporally extended process-subject from inception to just prior to its satisfaction. Its satisfaction is not a whole but an object, the "privileged" *part* in the next whole.

initial objectified and prehended situation as a "datum," rather than "data" (for example, the Category of Explanation xvii, *PR* 24).

This datum is felt simultaneously by an actual entity as a complex group, a non-personal nexus, objectified in the new actual entity as its "actual world" for its new coming-to-be. When he is emphasizing the process as a growing together, a "concrescence" of the many (of the world's multiplicity of satisfaction/superjects), he uses the term "data" (for example, *PR* 30 and 40), though he is not consistent with this usage. "The 'universe' comprising the absolutely initial *data* for an actual entity is a multiplicity" (*PR* 30, emphasis added).

In *Adventures of Ideas* Whitehead, again, seeks to explain the origin of an actual entity's creative power that simultaneously grasps the multiplicity as one complex datum. "[T]he processes of the past, in their perishing, are themselves energizing as the complex origin of each novel occasion" (*AI* 276).

In *Process and Reality* he overstates this universal theory of relativity: "if we allow for degrees of relevance, and for negligible relevance, we must say that every actual entity is present in every other actual entity" (*PR* 50), and again, "It has become a 'being'; and it belongs to the nature of every 'being' that it is a potential for every 'becoming'" (*PR* 45).

In later works he corrects this exaggeration: "The data for any one pulsation of actuality consist of the full content of the *antecedent* universe as it exists in relevance to that pulsation" (*MT* 89, emphasis added), and "The whole antecedent world conspires to produce a new occasion" (*MT* 164). And for an even stronger denial: "It is not true that whatever happens is immediately a condition laid upon everything else. Such a conception of complete mutual determination is an exaggeration of the community of the Universe" (*AI* 198).

Before examining how the Categories handle universal relativity, more insight as to the origin of an actual entity's activity, its creativity, might be found by looking again at the Category of the Ultimate. Perhaps the concern with the source of the creative wholeness of each moment lies within an inadequate understanding of the Category of the Ultimate itself. Is the origin of a moment's creative energy any more mysterious than the action of creativity itself?

Basic Anatomy of an Actual Entity

THE ULTIMATE CATEGOREAL DIPOLARITY BETWEEN A WHOLE AND ITS PARTS

Whitehead's famous formulation of the Ultimate Category is terse and quotable, but not without a major equivocation that affects how much of his metaphysical system is to be interpreted. In "The many become one and are increased by one," what does Whitehead mean by "one?" Since he does not ascribe to absolute simples (though some might say that his "eternal objects" come close), the basic ones in his system are actual entities (Category of Existence i, *PR* 22). "One" should be identified with an actual entity and an actual entity with a "whole," and a whole with the process from prehended data to satisfaction, for example: "This final decision is the reaction of the unity of the *whole* to its own internal determination (*PR* 28, emphasis added)," and "the impossibility of understanding its [satisfaction's] generation without recourse to the whole subject" (*PR* 221).

Yet, there is also good reason to believe, as many Whitehead scholars do, that a "whole" is what the actual entity ends up creating, since he often says as much, and probably even in his characterization of the Ultimate Category. This implies that the result of the actual entity is the one and, therefore, the whole. This interpretation is strongly suggested by Whitehead's characterization of the creative process as a "concrescence" implying that the many are growing together into a single unit which is finally achieved at its satisfaction. This popular understanding of the nature of an actual entity is, in my estimation, wrong, whatever Whitehead is finally taken to say. It raises problems that have no elegant answers, amongst which is the origin of creativity and what "creativity" really means. It seems ultimately to deny coming-to-be is primary with being subordinated to process in the dipolar units of reality.

The ambiguity hinges on the meaning of "become." "Become" is mainly used in a process context as a synonym for "coming-to-be" and thereby contrasted to "being" as something that is or has come to be; so when Whitehead says that "the many become one," it implies the many are not one during concrescence. Only at the end do they stop becoming one and simply are one. Further, what does he mean by the many "are increased by one"? Does he mean there is a new actual entity, a new subjective whole after the becoming? Not likely, though I think this should be what he means. He seems to say there is a new object, a new being that has come to be—one more being in being—a being that would contain the many beings

43

the concrescing actual entity began with, though with modifications, modifications which can even include, it seems for Whitehead, eliminations.

What if we allow "become" to be used also as a term for "transition" as well as "process"? Occasionally Whitehead uses "become" for "transition:" "'memory' is a very special instance of an antecedent act of experience *becoming* a datum of intuition for another act of experience" (*PR* 142, emphasis added); and alternatively he has used the term "transition" to refer to "concrescence": "The 'formal' constitution of an actual entity is a process of *transition* from indetermination towards terminal determination" (*PR* 45, emphasis added). But if an actual entity is a whole, not just coordinately, but temporally, then it is temporally one from its beginning until it stops creating. It is always, throughout its creative life, a singular dipolar unit. It is also spatially one, that is, all that are prehended simultaneously set up a complex coordinated contrast, but it is one coordinate complex, a unity with many contrasts; they are the "datum" with its given patterned qualities.

An actual entity is temporally one because there is only one process of creativity from beginning to end. Since the many of the data are all in the actual entity when it begins, and since the creative process is one unit or creative epoch from beginning to end, when Whitehead says the "many become one," he should be referring to the very inception of the actual entity. More accurately, the many become/are parts of the new dipolar one. The parts provide the potentiality for the moment that the creativity tries to fulfill in some way. The creativity of the moment is *not* a "growing together" (concrescence) of the inherited many; they are all together in the one actual entity from the beginning. "The objectified particular occasions together have the unity of a datum for the creative concrescence" (*PR* 210). Creativity can only adjust the significance of items in the datum.

Creativity, the subjective "oneness" of the dipolar whole, works at making a new being, but the new being, as with any being, is never a whole. Being is only one in abstraction from the whole it is in. *The satisfaction of a moment is never dipolar; and nothing exists except dipolar actual entities.* The created being is always a part in a new whole (or wholes), one of which must begin immediately as the prior whole ceases with its "privileged" gift of being for the new whole.

The Category of the Ultimate should read something like: Many beings are (become) parts of one whole that is becoming a new part for successive wholes. Whitehead also has an expression that captures the necessity for every successful process to end in another process: "The creature perishes

Basic Anatomy of an Actual Entity

and is immortal" (*PR* 82, Whitehead's emphasis). Immortality requires the perished coming-to-be to be (a being) in another actual entity, and so on forever.

Though it is true that every being will be inherited by many, even in an unending sequence of comings-to-be, the being that comes to be during the creative process *must* be followed by one unique, process that immediately inherits its predecessors superject as its "privileged" being/datum: the one that closes up the prior coming-to-be with no temporal gap between the satisfied end and the new whole's beginning. The necessity for a new whole to follow *every* new determination created by a whole is no less basic than the necessity for every whole to be a process. It is just the transition side of the Category of the Ultimate.

To use Whitehead's misleading language, a "concrescence" cannot reach a determinate result unless a new concrescence "accepts" the being created by the prior process. It is "in the nature of things" that a new creating whole begins with a prior's creation. And since it "belongs to the essential constitution of each such occasion" that it have a "creative urge" (*AI* 193), any attempt to find why it is so, must appeal to explanations that are less basic than the Category of the Ultimate and will only raise other questions. Appeals to God/dess, for example, as the source of creativity, rather than seeing the cosmic Wholes as supreme embodiments of the Ultimate Principle, will fail to explain how it is possible God/dess can so act. If we in the end come to an end of explanation, at least we must attempt to minimize, hopefully to one inexplicable, the ultimate starting point of explanation in order to avoid arbitrary dualities and incoherencies.

THE INITIAL DATUM AND THE THEORY OF RELATIVITY

> It is not true that whatever happens is immediately a condition laid upon everything else. Such a conception of complete mutual determination is an exaggeration of the community of the Universe (*AI* 198).

When Whitehead says (without adding the word "antecedent"), "if we allow for degrees of relevance, and for negligible relevance, we must say that every actual entity is present in every other actual entity" (*PR* 50), he is not just adopting Anaxagoras' position that the same *kinds* of qualities are found in all the seeds (atoms). For Whitehead, each unique individual moment is included in all (successive) moments—always with the understanding that it is the moment's accomplishment that is found in others, not its creative effort, not the processing whole. Anaxagoras, too, excepted *nous*, mind, from the (infinite) divisibility that characterized his seeds. Even though Whitehead does not make the mistake of assuming contrasts imply divisibility, as so many have since Anaxagoras, the contrasts displayed by the initial datum do not exist apart from the subject that is simultaneously everywhere in the spatially extended actuality and so feels all its parts simultaneously. The creative mentality is the same undivided, mental whole that survives continuously from the actual entity's inception to its satisfaction. So, given the clarifications (1) that there can be no mutual prehensions between actual entities in process, and (2) that only prior actual*ized* actual entities can be in successive actual entities, Whitehead does assert that "Each atom is a system of all things" (*PR* 36).

What really is in the initial phase of an actual entity? How can the "whole antecedent world" be available for each actual entity? Can it really "belong to the nature of every 'being' that it is a potential for *every* 'becoming'" (*PR* 22, emphasis added), even understood to mean every new becoming? What does this mean for Whitehead's doctrine of "negative prehension?" And how can passive beings "conspire?"

An actual entity begins and remains (as long as it is creating) a dipolar entity. There is not first the process and then the process inheriting beings. Neither are there beings and then a process that includes them. Beings don't exist apart from their inclusion as the subordinate pole of the process-being dipolarity in at least one actual entity. Likewise, process, the dynamic whole, is meaningless unless it has parts. The parts are the potency but only relative to a whole; the whole is the actualizing of the potency; with no beings to "carry" the potency, no actualizing is possible. "In this way there is constituted the concrescent subject in its primary phase with its dipolar constitution, physical and mental, indissoluble" (*PR* 244).

No actual entity can reach a satisfied determination on its own. The "satisfaction" is not *in* the actual entity that creates it. The subject that creates the new being never feels it. The determination an actual entity makes must fall in the lap of another or it is not yet a determinate being. That a moment can become satisfied and wait for another to find it is also wrong. A satisfaction is a being, and all beings are potencies; but potentiality is only meaningful as the subordinate pole of a dipolar entity. However, once in being, "the oneness of each element in the universe [must be repeated]

Basic Anatomy of an Actual Entity

... to the crack of doom in the creative advance from creature to creature" (*PR* 228). Parmenides may have erred in denying the creation of new being is possible, but he was on very solid ground when he pointed out that being cannot be altered or eliminated. Once something is, it is as it is forever. Reality's "whole history" may not reside in each non-divine whole, but a locus must eventually be found for the reality of the past, what it means to be "past" and, further, what it means to be "the complete past."

POTENTIALITY AS THE SUBJECTIVE AIM

Each atom is a system of all things (*PR* 36).

The Category of the Ultimate should be understood to say that an actual entity can only reach its determinate goal by being a datum for, or in, another dipolar moment: Determinateness is always a conditioning of a whole by a part, so what an actual entity creates can only exist in another whole. It does not follow, however, that the new creating whole with its "privileged" determination, includes only data from this one prior determination. Every moment must be creating something new or it does not exist. When Whitehead says inorganic occasions lack mentality, he can only be speaking hyperbolically (*MT* 62). Even the expression "create something new" is a redundancy since "to create" means "to make something new." To create something new requires the real potentiality for something new to occur. Potentiality is being (as embraced by a whole). One being, the being just created and embraced by the next moment, cannot, alone, offer anything new for the "new" moment. It is what it is; and what it is has already been created.

However, the initiation of a new moment does not occur relative to just one included being, one prior actualization. Each actual entity comes into existence in a social environment. Some have just come to be; others are coming to be and as processes sustain the beings they have inherited. There may be processes that overlap and include the same beings that the new moment under consideration does; however, they must include or exclude some others it doesn't. Unless the new occasion is a member of the lowest-level society in its cosmic epoch, it will also overlap and prehend contiguous beings brought into being by occasions of less inclusive scope and creative ability; it will probably also prehend, though with more vagueness, creations by those higher in the hierarchy than itself.

Finally, during every moment a cosmic Whole creates a new comic Being. This Being is everywhere and so must be included in every new process, including the next cosmic Whole. It must be included as part of the "actual[ized] world" founding every process. Just because a process has included a being in its initial data does not make that being unavailable to other processes. Beings are and remain public even as they are included in, and condition, the subjectivity of an actual entity. They are not just accessible; they are necessarily embraced by every nascent actual entity that occurs contiguous and successive to them. Again, an actual entity cannot terminate as a determinate, satisfied being unless it occurs "in" a new actual entity founded upon that "privileged" superject, plus others in its immediate neighborhood.

Though a new actual entity, N, must start immediately with the satisfaction of its predecessor, M, this is not true of beings in its immediate neighborhood created by others. Say a neighbor, P, has created a being that is part of a new moment, Q. N must not only inherit what M created, but must inherit what P created so long as it is sustained in being by Q and N is contiguous to the being P created for Q, even if Q begins before N. N's neighbors' creations must be prehended so long as a neighbor created it before N begins and is maintained by a contemporary process that is contiguous to where N begins.

Since reality must be a multiplicity of creators, every actual entity is not just founded on its own predecessor that provides its privileged datum, but on all those less inclusive and more inclusive that sustain a being within the regional standpoint of the newly founded creative whole. A being (once created) remains forever part of some processes or other and is accessible to all new moments that "overlap it" "to the crack of doom."

Whitehead calls potentiality that arises from an actualized world, "real potentiality," as opposed to "pure potentiality" which is not conditioned by prior actuality. In terms of the Categories suggested for the metaphysical scheme presented here, "pure potentiality" is a meaningless expression since nothing can exist unless it begins with prior determinations, that is, with prior actualized entities that have created beings to be the potentiality for others that succeed them. So the actualized actual entities around which new actualities begin are as much opportunities as they are limitations on possible creations. Without prior beings, no potentiality for any outcome exists. Creativity can bring a new determination into being in innumerable ways within the range of the unique aim provided by the datum because all potentiality exists as a continuum allowing endless possible ways (be they trivially different) to be specified no matter how restricted the range of opportunity is that is inherited.

CREATIVITY AND ITS AIMS

The transition side of the Category of the Ultimate requires an actual entity to begin just as its successful predecessor ends in order that its predecessor can be objectified as a satisfied determination. This actual entity that is initiated with its predecessor's privileged superject also includes any other beings that other actual entities are sustaining in its neighborhood. All these beings form the subordinate pole of the new dipolar actuality. Because there is a novel combination of others, a unique potentiality is established, but only if the inclusive pole, the subjective activity of the whole, also exists to actualize the potentiality. This creativity of the moment is the universal urge to novelty. An actual entity must bring about a new being, or, in the case of some fragmentary occasions of intermediate complexity, fail trying. But novelty is merely anything different from the immediate past of the actual entity in question. Every actual entity is also provided with a general direction to proceed while creating the novelty. This goal is the moment's "subjective aim."

The most general aim, the aim that is universal and unavoidable, is the "objective aim." Whitehead calls it "The generic aim of process . . ." which in this passage he gives as "the attainment of importance . . ." (*MT* 12). It, like all metaphysical principles, was never created, but has always been a necessary aspect of every actual entity. It is "objective" because it is, and always has been, an "object" for every actual entity as it prehends its initial datum because every being created carries with it the universal purpose of existence. This ultimate purpose is seldom articulated, and an argument can be mounted that no one has clearly done so. Only actual entities with some consciousness are able to attempt to express what the universal purpose is. If they do so inadequately and try to act as if it were the way reality must be, they will be living with an internal conflict, a conflict not felt by actual occasions that have no choice but to blindly fulfill the aim in some way or other.

To fully understand what the purpose of existence is, is to articulate a full metaphysic, but for now, say this purpose is to enrich reality, that is, to contribute what is created to One that can evaluate every contribution against all others, and to One who cannot lose anything that is ever created. Such a One will necessarily be the oneness of a personal series of Actual Entities, not just one actual entity. The actual entities in this personal series will in their turn be enriching all other actual occasions because the world's occasions must prehend as data these enriched and enriching Person's creations.

In order to fulfill the universal aim, it must be felt by a subject with creative power feeling its datum as potency. The objective aim, therefore, is the most generic aspect of every subjective aim. Since every aspect of the initial datum is felt subjectively, the subjective aim needn't be provided by any other means than the data itself. One could say that God/dess supplies the aim at each moment to each actual entity because the divine personal series has always fulfilled the universal generic aim, and so has always exhibited and presented the aim to every successive actual entity as it prehends the most recent cosmic Being. Every item of the multiplicity (felt as the initial datum) carries all the unavoidable metaphysical characteristics including the objective aim as each actual entity has particularized it.

The subjective aim is the objective aim particularized to be absolutely unique for each moment. It is possible some, if not most, of the multiplicity in its datum is also found in the initial data of other subjects, but never exactly the same collection. Since the specific includes the general, it is possible that others can feel the same feelings at a higher level of generality, but each actual entity begins with a once-in-the-universe opportunity and creates a determination that in its full details has never existed before. What it specifies in its determination is not fully specified in some realm of possibilities waiting to be made actual by way of "ingression." A particular determinate specification is only possible once. It is what "actualized" means.

An actual entity's subjective aim must be totally relevant to its content. The only way this can happen is for the aim to incorporate all the uniqueness of the initial data. The completely particularized aim that is relevant to each actual entity is a social outcome. Not even God/dess' latest Being can contain the exact data contrasts that establishes a particular actual occasion. Actual occasions, whose processes end at nearly the same time as the latest divine creation, can provide data for a new occasion *simultaneously* with God/dess' contribution, so the occasion has data from its environs that has not yet been created into a cosmic Being (has not yet become part of a divine satisfaction/superject), and so it cannot be part of the latest cosmic Being that contributes to the multiplicity of beings the new occasion has for

Basic Anatomy of an Actual Entity

its initial data. Every initial multiplicity is a unique once-in-the-universe multiplicity that cannot be found in some realm of "eternal" objects in the divine mentality. Only the objective aim is eternal and always the same everywhere, as are all metaphysical conditions.

The subjective aim is somewhat generic; though it is the least generic range of potentiality incorporating all the aspects of the initial datum. If further specification were not possible, no creating could take place. It's a range of potentiality not all of which is equally probable. The likelihood of fulfillment somewhere along the continuum will exhibit a statistical curve.

Neither can the subjective aim be a multiplicity of fully specified options (eternal objects) one of which the actual entity chooses: The multiplicity of the "completely initial data" cannot be a singular subjective aim. The subjective aim is the unity of the subject, the unity of the process. Creating is not merely choosing nor concrescing; it creates the options to choose; it is "the actualization of potentiality . . ." (*AI* 179), which makes more sense as specifying than choosing, especially when the doctrine of a multiplicity of "eternal objects" is abandoned in favor of potentiality as a continuum. The only "choice" a moment makes is to stop creating options, at which point the moment perishes either as the privileged datum for a new actual entity or dies before it can reach a satisfaction because no tolerable options for further determinate specification could be created within the generic range presented to the occasion.

Every actual*ized* actual entity is an everlasting being, more or less complex, but always one member of a multiplicity of beings others must simultaneously inherit. The multiplicity of beings is the result of many satisfied, contemporaneous actual entities' creative processes. No one of the multiplicity chooses the collective outcome. Neither does the actual entity (that contains the many superjects) choose which are in and which are not: If a being resides contiguous to where a new actual entity begins, it must be included.

STRUCTURED QUALITIES AS INITIAL DATA

The initial data for the new actual entity has both spatial order, that is, coordinate relationships, as well as kinds and degrees of emotional urgency, that is, the objectified multiplicity has both structure and qualities. Every datum will provide qualities in a pattern. The pattern, presented by the mutually externally related qualities of contemporaneous processes as actualized, however vague, shows where each member of the contemporaneous multiplicity of processes was relative to others before they perished as actualized. Neither the quantitative structure nor the qualities are created by the "concrescence" of the inheriting actual entity. It is "given" to the dipolar, nascent moment as its subordinate pole. These beings are feelings, the exact feelings the prior actual entities felt as they reached their satisfied determinations. "[T]he subjective forms of the immediate past are continuous [not "reproduced" as Whitehead often says] with those of the present" (*AI* 183). These feelings carry imbedded feelings of even earlier moments which provide the meaning of "temporal order." "To be a part of" is to be "earlier than" even though all parts are present in the present, directly or mediated. The structure of spatial order is simultaneity. "All together," none as a part of another, though all as parts in the present, is the general meaning of "spatial extension."

RELATIVITY AND THE SUBJECTIVE AIM

Even the simplest possible actual entity inherits more than one other simultaneously. Does it inherit the whole antecedent world which Whitehead says "conspires to produce a new occasion" (*MT* 164)? Apart from the metaphorical, if not mythical, use of "conspires," how can it happen "that every being is a potential for every becoming" (*PR* 22)? The answer is partly in what Whitehead wrote just before this quote: "every item in *its* universe is involved in each concrescence" (*PR* 22, emphasis added), so "every being" means "every being in its universe" which I have suggested means every prior being that lies contiguously to the incipient actuality, and this is always more than the one being whose satisfaction establishes the new, privileged datum for the immediately successive actual entity. This need for multiple, simultaneous inheritances is contrary to Whitehead's suggestion that

> In two extreme cases the initial data of a feeling have a unity of their own. In one case, the data reduce to a single actual entity, other than the subject of the feeling; and in the other case the data reduce to a single eternal object (*PR* 231).

"Eternal objects" as the source of potency is problematic, but prehending an eternal object on its own apart from its being embedded in a created subject/superject is even more so. Certainly, if prehending one actual

Basic Anatomy of an Actual Entity

entity's superject could initiate a new actual entity, there would definitely be a need to also supply the new process with a subjective aim in addition to the single datum since the single datum would provide no new potency.

Every actual entity must include several fragmentary others' superjects as well as the privileged datum that closed up the prior process. There is also always the latest cosmic Being that no new actuality can avoid including because this Being is ubiquitous and so is part of the "actual world" of every coming-to-be subsequently established. Many make much of the subjective aim being established by divine power, yet an aim must include the influence of one's immediate neighbors, that is, the initial data that prior and contiguous others have created, in addition to the last cosmic Being.

What more can be in the aim than these beings, one of which is the most recent cosmic Being? The initial data come to the new actual entity with spatial order and degrees of emotional qualities, as Whitehead also says, so "concrescence" doesn't generate the unity that establishes an actual entity:

> Thus the present is perceivable in so far as it is conditioned by the efficient causation from the past of the perceiver. The great dominant relationships, fundamental for the epochal order of nature, thereby stand out with overwhelming distinctness. These are the general, all-pervasive, obligations of perspective. Such relationships are what we term the spatial relationships as perceivable from the standpoint of the observer (*AI* 218) ... The relevant environment, which is the immediate past of the human body, is peculiarly sensitive to its geometrical experiences and to the synthesis of its qualitative prehensions with these experiences of geometrical relations. In that way, there is a basis in fact for the association of derivates from significant regions in the past with the geometrical representatives of those regions in the present (*AI* 218–219).

If an actual entity is one actuality in a personal series, the immediate successor of an actual entity of that individual is a "privileged" actual entity, that is, an actual entity that begins with the satisfaction of its predecessor. The superject of the privileged member's immediate predecessor is normally the most influential aspect in a privileged occasion's datum. However, this is only likely in personal societies contingently created at a level more enriched that those of the lowest-level society. The lowest-level society will have strands of personal order, since each member must end as the privileged datum for its immediate successor, but the members inheriting the privileged datum are no more enriched by this datum than they are by the data inherited from any other members of the society. For this reason, this lowest-level society is experienced as a non-personal society.

SUBJECTIVITY AND THE SUBJECTIVE AIM

Whitehead, in the following passage, gives his reason for requiring an actual entity to have a subjective aim in addition to the subjective forms given to an occasion as the objective data inherited from others:

> Thus a single occasion is alive [as opposed to inorganically enduring] when the subjective aim which determines its process of concrescence has introduced a novelty of definiteness not to be found in the inherited data of its primary phase. The novelty is introduced conceptually and disturbs the inherited "responsive" adjustment of subjective forms. It alters the "values," in the artist's sense of that term (*PR* 104).

Certainly, there would be no novelty in the new, "alive" occasion if it only inherited its datum from one prior occasion, but this is impossible. Even "The simplest grade of actual occasions must be conceived as experiencing a few sensa, with the minimum of patterned contrast" (*PR* 115). It begins with many beings created by many prior neighbors, including, in every case, the most recent, cosmically omnipresent Being. A single inherited being provides no uniqueness or novelty, but any combination of newly created beings must be novel. (I also hold that the novelty can be so overwhelming for some intermediately complex non-divine occasions in a personal nexus that they fail to achieve a new determination.)

Since being is potentiality, and since the dipolar actuality must feel all the beings in its "actual world" simultaneously, it must have a unique subjective feeling as a whole. This complex feeling must partially, if not largely, determine the outcome of the occasion's creativity simply because an occasion can only become what its potency provides and allows. The data influence, literally "flow into," the outcome. However, the potentiality of the inherited datum is always a *kind* of determination within which the moment must create a specific outcome. Even so, by itself, in abstraction from the whole it is in, the datum is not aimed at anything; it is passive. However, this abstraction is an abstraction, never the way actuality concretely is. The superject is always in a new dipolar whole whose creative impulse actualizes the given potency towards an end.

Basic Anatomy of an Actual Entity

Beings are potencies only because they are always a part of a dipolar actuality, the wholeness or unity of which is creativity. What can "creative activity" mean other than "doing something not done before?" This drive, expressed by the Category of the Ultimate, is the conceptual side or wholeness of the dipolar entity. When it does create a somewhat novel feeling, the feeling of the whole process unity is altered. Thus, there is always a direction, a vector, along which every actual entity must progress, namely, to leave the past, to be somewhat different from the past, and yet to do so, more specifically, along lines in keeping with the urgings from its inherited past.

Each divine creation, in keeping with the Categories proposed here, includes both the cosmic past, that is, the satisfied Actual Entities of the primordial cosmic nexus, and the world's fragmentary creations, but only those that have already come to be when the new cosmically inclusive coming-to-be begins. No matter how rapidly the members of the cosmic personal series process to a new determinations, there will always be determinate beings created by non-divine occasions in the actualized world of every nascent actual occasion that are not yet parts of the next divine actualization but are parts of that nascent occasion's initial data.[6]

So for those who agree with the Hartshornean view expressed here that the divine's creations are prehended by all subsequent actual entities, it is both true and misleading to say divinity establishes an actual entity's aim, misleading because the latest member of the divine nexus is not the only contributor to the initial data that forms the initial aims for fragmentary occasions. The latest divine satisfaction/superject cannot even be the complete aim for the next divine Whole (because the world's superjects must also contribute to the aim of each divine process), but the divine's latest creation does provide a part of all aims established subsequent to its creation. Its ubiquitous presence assures the universe has a minimal order whereby the positive dominates no matter how much disruption there is.

---

6 Another approach would be to take the somewhat arbitrary position, as I once did, that all fragmentary occasions must end as a cosmically inclusive actual entity begins, so each moment of divinity is always immediately inclusive of all the beings there are ("Hartshorne, God and Metaphysics: How the Cosmically Inclusive Personal Nexus and the World Interact" *Process Studies* 28/3–4 (1999) 212–30). But even with this approach, there are fragmentary superjects that are not contiguous to a particular moment (that is, not part of a particular occasion's initial data) because even though God/dess is experiencing them, they are not yet part of the latest divine Being and so cannot yet affect the world's occasions, nor have these superjects been transmitted to the fragmentary moment's contiguous neighborhood by mediating, fragmentary occasions.

Since every being is a vector, coming from somewhere with anticipation it will become part of the present's conditioning of others beyond itself, every being felt is part of one's aim. Since the Being that is all-inclusive and non-fragmentary is also everywhere present, this cosmic reality is a factor in every aim. But reality is necessarily social; no one is, or does, all of anything. This is true even of divinity when the focus is on coming-to-be rather than what has come to be. Reality, understood as what is in process, is irreducibly a multiplicity; here even cosmic reality is "one among many" (*MT* 110). When Whitehead wrote, "The ultimate metaphysical truth is atomism" (*PR* 35), he may have been referring only to the temporal extent or epoch of each moment, but it is true also of any cross-section or duration of the universe: Reality is irreducibly a multiplicity of processes, each its own "atom" of self-creating, even if others overlap much of the same initial data.

If divine power alone were posited to establish each aim, rather than holding that the subjective aim is objectified as the initial datum itself, what would establish the divine aims? All attempts to answer this question make God/dess an exception to the metaphysical principles. Such approaches come down to having a power establish the Categories themselves, and while so doing necessarily function in a way that does not require the so-called "necessary" principles of the Categoreal Scheme. Metaphysics, as the study of the unavoidable, reappears, then, as creation by divine fiat, as contingent, not necessary.

Chapter 5

Comparing Whitehead's Categoreal Obligations

WHITEHEAD'S CATEGOREAL OBLIGATIONS SHOULD be further unavoidable specifications of the Category of the Ultimate, but they are really a mixture of metaphysical necessities and contingent principles actual occasions may use to enhance reality's aesthetic richness. Only those principles necessarily exhibited by the two necessary societies (the lowest-level non-personal society and the unsurpassable personal Society) can be strictly metaphysical. Some of the differences between the metaphysical scheme being outlined here and Whitehead's Categoreal Scheme will be pointed out in the following discussion of his Categoreal Obligations (*PR* 26–28).

The Category of Subjective Unity, i, which requires every actual entity to finish satisfied once begun, makes "death" of a personal nexus impossible to rationalize.[7] It can and must apply to actual entities in the two necessary societies, but cannot necessarily apply to mid-level personal societies, all of which will eventually die because they exist contingently. What this Category can mean is: Every actual entity begins as a dipolar whole with an aim provided by the inherited actual world within a creative, dipolar whole that projects hope for a new determinate actualization that will and must include the data.

But in only two cases is it a necessity that an initiated actual entity end with that hope fulfilled: Either, (1) by a personal nexus with supreme

---

7. More on this later when discussing "death," in chapter 10.

power and flexibility capable of tolerating any possible state of affairs the world can create, or (2) by a non-personal society whose members are so innocuously bland and similar as to never produce enough diversity to challenge the creative ability of *all* its members and so will always have some members or other existing.

The Categories of Objective Identity and Diversity, ii and *iii* simply state the metaphysical truth that the datum is, and must remain, the datum it is. The transition to a new actual entity cannot change it, nor can "concrescence" change it since each item of the objective datum must find its place in the eventual satisfaction (*PR* 26). Despite Whitehead's speaking of process (concrescence) as integrating the initial data, the diversity of the data must come to a new actual entity not in serial form but coordinately. This implies that the spatial, quantitative relationships of the data are also given, not just their qualitative feelings. "Integration" can only mean, (1) "adjustment of the significance" of the elements in the datum, or (2) adding newly created feelings; it cannot mean "putting the inherited feelings together coordinately" or "dismissing them" completely. "Thus, the supervention of the later phase[s] does not involve elimination by negative prehensions" (*PR* 240).

The Category of Conceptual Valuation, iv, also called *Conceptual Reproduction* (*PR* 26, 33, 101, 316) is a metaphysical necessity if it means that the dipolar actual entity feels as a whole what the parts bring to the whole. There is not first the physical feeling and then a (reproduced) conceptual feeling. *All feeling is conceptual*: Only wholes feel. The initial wholeness of the actual entity feels as it does because is feels the inherited parts as they are. What makes these feelings "physical" is their inalterability expressed by the Categories of Objective Identity and Diversity. Societies are composed of discrete moments; they are spatial-temporal "atoms." What holds societies together is not the *reproduction* of feeling, but the identity of feeling. The same feeling that ends a moment is simply felt by a superseding whole that includes that prior feeling, the privileged datum, along with others.

Whitehead's analysis of "transition" sometimes suggests transition is a process:

> The "initial data" constitute a "multiplicity." . . There is a concrescence of the initial data into the objective datum made possible by the elimination [via negative prehension] . . . The objective [objectified] datum is the perspective of the initial data (*PR* 221).

Transition is never a temporally extended process; it is simultaneously the end of one process whole and the beginning of another. "Thus perishing is the initiation of becoming. How the past perishes is how the future [present?] becomes" (*AI* 238). "[T]he subjective forms of the immediate past are *continuous* with those of the present" (*AI* 183, emphasis added). "Saying an actual entity "becomes" part of another is misleading. An actual*ized* entity simply "is" a part of another that is its successor. To say the satisfaction must occur "before" it can be a part of another is misleading; there is no temporal order here. It is just as true to say that the beginning of the new process is the end of the prior process as it is to say the end of a process whole is the beginning of another.

When stating the "principle of relativity," Whitehead vacillates between saying every item in *the* universe (*PR* 41) is involved in the concrescence of an actual entity, and every item in *its* universe (*PR* 22), but in the Categories proposed here, it cannot mean the elimination of any data that are prior and contiguous to the new actual entity. Neither can "negative prehending" be a metaphysical necessity if it means elimination of data prehended from actual entities contiguous to the nascent actual entity. Whitehead himself seems to say a "negative prehension" is merely a matter of emphasis since he writes, "In fact if we allow for degrees of relevance, and for negligible relevance, we must say that every actual entity is present in every other actual entity" (*PR* 50). This statement is hyperbole only in that it collapses an "actual entity" (which is a whole, a spatial-temporally extended creative process) and an "actual*ized* entity" (which is a changeless part in other successive actual entities). It also ignores necessary temporal ordering: An actual entity that is actualized after a prior actualization cannot be a part in the prior's process. This statement (*PR* 50) seems compatible with the doctrine of completely "windowed monads" that must accept into feeling, with some degree of relevance, everything in their actual worlds (E2a): "Each atom is a system of all things" (*PR* 36) of its actual*ized* environment.

Even if Whitehead means by "negative prehension" that an actual occasion's standpoint in the world requires that entity to have only some prior creations available as initial data, why say perspective requires action to eliminate the non-contiguous data? There is no temporal extension between the dipolar feeling an actual entity has just before it reaches a satisfaction and the feeling felt by the next subject of the datum. Many problems arise if one proposes there is temporal extension between the creation of a satisfaction as "initial data" and its inclusion in a new process as its "objective datum." Other beings in other contiguous subjects will be in, or sustained by, those processes prior to being prehended as additional parts of an actual entity's objective datum.

To have a perspective merely means that an actual occasion is not contiguous to, or does not overlap, all the beings there are. The actual occasion contains some, not all, and is, therefore, a "fragment" (to use Hartshorne's term) of all there is. Only one actual entity at each moment can logically have no perspective and, therefore, be all-inclusive.

Though a boundary occurs between wholes, process does not cease. The boundary is an unalterable condition made by one actual entity that exists, as actualized, only as a part immediately felt by another. There is, of course, a temporal ordering of the two comings-to-be, but transition is not temporally extended. Wholes are atomic, but the process of a whole is continuous, and where the creativity of one whole ends, another whole begins, but since process without its other dipolar element (namely, being), is not a whole, "it" in itself cannot be given an ordered designation as can wholes. "Creativity" does not need to come from someplace as the new whole begins; it is there as the inclusive dipolar pole of the former and its privileged successor. There is no break in creativity at transition; it is continuous both within a whole and from one whole to another.

Though every successful whole can only be successful as the privileged datum in new whole, no whole feels just this one prior actualization. It feels its whole neighborhood, a multiplicity of beings. It feels all the members of this multiplicity simultaneously, so the many are felt as one complex datum which in itself is changeless, unique and suggestive of a *kind* of outcome for the new moment. The changelessness is the stubbornness of the past; the uniqueness establishes the novelty required for a new creation; and the possibility for new specification arises because the vectored datum presents a generic continuum, that is, "real potentiality" that can be further specified.

The complete datum is both the subject's past, *and* its aim for the future. The dipolar subject feels the past, but always vectored as a means to an end. Since it must feel all the elements of the datum simultaneously, it is always evaluating, throughout its process, the significance of one aspect against others. This gradually alters the way the subject feels the past by *adding* new feeling(s) to the whole: "The novelty [of the subjective aim] is introduced conceptually and disturbs the inherited 'responsive' adjustment of subjective forms. It alters the 'values,' in the artist's sense of that term" (*PR* 104). However, Whitehead might better have said the aim is introduced objectively, since ultimate purpose arrives as a metaphysical necessary with the objective data, and the particularized aim for each moment arrives as the full contingent uniqueness of each moment's datum.

The Category of Conceptual Reversion, v, Whitehead eventually dismisses as metaphysically unnecessary (PR 250) because when God's storehouse of eternal objects is considered, all Reversion is then seen as the physical (hybrid physical) feeling of objects in God, namely, "ingression." However, in terms of the scheme suggested here, Reversion is the very meaning of "creativity." Reversion, which should be seen as creative origination, is a necessary characteristic of every actual entity. If creativity is to be taken seriously, it must bring forth something newly specified. That newness is the generation of somewhat new feelings, not the ingression of eternally specified feelings.

Potentiality is not a realm different from being: It is being as couched in a dipolar whole, and, as Whitehead says, being "is a potential for every 'becoming,'" at least for every becoming that must include it. The actual entity does not need to reproduce the feelings of its datum; it has them all. It must, however, work at creating a somewhat new feeling for its immediate successor (and others that will include it), a new feeling not even found in the divine's "primordial nature." Depending on the creative power of the moment, it will be more or less like the datum. This is why the new feelings will be, as Whitehead says, relevant to, or guided by, the subjective aim since the "subjective aim" is the immediate feeling of the data, including the metaphysically objective purpose felt subjectively and particularized by the uniqueness of the data.

The Category of Transmutation, vi, is definitely not metaphysically general. The cosmically inclusive person cannot use it because it obscures facts as they are, and the lowest-level society does not use it because its members are not creative enough to do so. Principles that are interesting, but not metaphysically general will be discussed in the chapters on contingent social organization, chapters 10–13.

The Category of Subjective Harmony, vii, states that any adjustments to the feelings in the process whole will be made within the range of the initial subjective aim and relevant to any additional feelings generated by the internal creativity of the process. Since the subjective aim is the initial data felt as one complex set of contrasts including the objective aim, and since any newly generated feelings must spring from prior feelings, all feelings will be related, usually enough so that a new determinate satisfaction is achievable within the continuum. Further, this Category points out that there is no such thing as a real multiplicity of feelings within a whole; this would imply a multiplicity of feelers. The whole may inherit many feelings, but as felt by a whole there is only one complex feeling.

> By the first categoreal condition the feelings of the earlier phase are compatible for integration. Thus the supervention of the later phase does not involve elimination by negative prehensions; such eliminations of positive prehensions in the concrescent subject would divide that subject into many subjects, and would divide these many subjects from the superject. But, though there can be no elimination from the supervening phase as a whole, there may be elimination from some *new* integral feeling which is merely one component of that phase (*PR* 240, emphasis added).

A feeling generated during the actual entity's creative process can be rejected, but all inherited feelings must be maintained with some degree of significance up to and including their inclusion in the final determination of the satisfaction, assuming the occasion is ordered enough to reach a satisfaction, that is, assuming it does not die before reaching a new determination.

Each feeling is part of the whole's singular, though likely complex, feeling. Every part contributes to the whole's feeling the feeling it does because it is a feeling a prior actual entity created for the world beyond itself; but its significance in the whole depends *partly* on its context within the whole. This is certainly a metaphysical necessity. Ignoring this truth commits the Aesthetic Fallacy. If the whole determined the feelings of its initial parts, the reality of the past would be lost.

As the whole processes towards a new determination, new, additional feeling is generated and added to the changeless past. (It is these *new* feelings that may be eliminated during the same process.) Any reference to a multiplicity of feelings in the whole abstracts from the singular, complex feeling that is the subjectivity of the whole. However, an analysis of aspects of the whole while ignoring the whole context will not produce error if the level of abstraction of the analysis is kept in mind. "Of course, whatever we can do in the way of abstraction is for some purposes useful—provided that we know what we are about" (*AI* 219). Whenever "feelings," as a plurality, are mentioned within one actual entity, one should be aware that an abstraction has taken place. The creating subject has only one complex feeling.

The Category of Subjective Intensity, viii, points out that the "real potentiality" provided by the founding datum is graded. The potentiality found in an actual entity always comes within a range of possible outcomes. However, an actualization within some region of the range is more likely than others. Given every actual entity's creative freedom, its outcome is only statistically predictable. Every process feels potentiality's vectors as anticipations of possible outcomes, possible outcomes that are more likely in the present or near future than in some distant future because, as one projects into the future, the potentiality in the present and near future becomes diluted or readjusted by the new potentiality provided by the future's additional determinations[8] because there must always be new data in future actualities. A personal nexus with consciousness can deliberately control somewhat the present and near future outcomes; with that element of control comes some responsibility for which outcomes do occur. Since nondivine persons need not be conscious, moral decision is not a metaphysical necessity; the statistical nature of potentialities' satisfactions, however, is a necessary condition of reality.

The Category of Freedom and Determination, ix, is likely Whitehead's best example of a dipolarly stated Category. Neither "freedom" nor "determination" makes sense without the other; yet they do not exist as equals. In terms of parts and wholes, freedom characterizes the whole, while all its inherited parts are settled and changeless causes in the whole. They determine the whole to be (somewhat) the whole it is, but the whole is always more than the disjunctive sum of its parts. Without this more, the parts would have nothing to determine; yet without the determinate parts, the whole would have no potentiality.

> [H]owever far the sphere of efficient causation be pushed in the determination of components of a concrescence . . . beyond the determination of these components there always remains the final reaction of the self-creative unity of the universe (*PR* 47).

The parts both limit what the whole can become and offer opportunities for it to take advantage of. The parts are inside the whole, but in the language of relations, the parts are externally related to the whole since the whole cannot alter them, while the whole is internally related to its parts since they condition what the whole can come to be.

8. The usual interpretation of chaos theory is to say the unknowability of the exact initial starting point determines the eventual outcome, but each moment adds its element of unpredictability. The "attractor" expresses the limits on the system's freedom.

Chapter 6

The Necessarily Existing Society of Perspectival Occasions

Minimally Creative Processes

In the actual world we discern four grades of actual occasions, grades which are not to be sharply distinguished from each other. First, and lowest, there are the actual occasions in so-called "empty space"; secondly, there are the actual occasions which are moments in the life-histories of enduring non-living objects, such as electrons or other primitive organisms; thirdly, there are the actual occasions which are moments in the life-histories of enduring living objects; fourthly, there are the actual occasions which are moments in the life-histories of enduring objects with conscious knowledge (*PR* 177–78)—[It's unfortunate that Whitehead didn't add a fifth, "God": it might have helped clarify whether he thought God was one actual entity or an "enduring object" composed of actual entities. His failure to address this is further evidence God is an afterthought to his system.]

NECESSITY AS A SOCIETAL FUNCTION

GIVEN THAT REALITY AT every level is composed of dipolar actual entities, and that every actual entity "perishes," and further that "absolute nothingness" is meaninglessness, what must exist? Much effort (mostly misplaced)

The Necessarily Existing Society of Perspectival Occasions

over the centuries has gone into trying to prove "God" must exist, but if actual entities are the only realities, and all actual entities are dipolar, something must exist each moment besides the creative activity of God/dess, namely, the subordinate pole of each of the divine dipolar acts. Each divine act requires a body to prehend, and this body can only be the world's creations in some form or other.

Every change (difference) signals that a new actual entity has occurred since each actual entity can only create one state of affairs. All actual entities' processes end either (1) by "dying" (perishing), leaving for others what they accomplished, or (2) failing to achieve a new determination. That each existed at all is not necessary; what each created was not necessary. All moments, including divine acts, are contingent in how they create. "Necessary existence" is not a property of dipolar wholes, not a property of individual actual entities.

However, not only does contingent change occur from moment to moment, created characteristics survive from one moment to the next. The actual entity originating and passing on the characteristic and the one that inherits the characteristic define a minimal "society." The differences and the survivals define an "event." So, two actual entities, one actualized and forming the primary (privileged) datum for the next actualization, define a minimally temporally extended event and an instance of a shortest surviving society.

If the defining characteristic could be the sole being inherited by a successor, a strict personal society would exist. But no satisfaction/superject alone can ever be the initial datum an actual entity inherits, so even personal societies are only more or less personal. Non-personal societies, likewise, are more or less non-personal. The characteristic defining a non-personal society is inherited by many occasions simultaneously, each of which may be a member in a subordinate society more or less personal. When many members of the society are then prehended simultaneously by an actual entity capable of extending over the many, a non-personal social nexus is experienced. If the prehending occasion is sufficiently creative, it may suppress the minor differences and experience the spatial region by its common characteristic alone, employing what Whitehead calls, the Category of Transmutation, a contingent function.

Obviously, societies survive longer than the actual entities that sustain them, but they only exist as long as new actual entities occur that do inherit the defining characteristic and successfully pass this inheritance on. What is not so obvious is whether any societies exist that must exist. Empirical evidence can establish there are very long-lasting societies, but necessities are the province of metaphysical investigation. Necessities are not created, nor can they ever cease, something empirical investigation cannot establish.

The Category of the Ultimate says an actual entity can only cease satisfied by creating a determination around which another begins its creative process. The successor is "privileged" because it is the only actual entity that must begin just as its predecessor ends. Other beings must also be prehended, but these others are maintained in existence by other actual entities that began somewhat earlier and are privileged relative to other predecessors.

Each dipolar process must have as its subordinate pole more objective data than that created by one prior actual entity since reality cannot exist as one strict personal nexus, namely, where one and only one actual entity prehends only one predecessor and perishes as the only being for the next actual entity. So even though the epochal process and transition of one actual entity after another forms a temporal strand of "privileged" personal order, reality is always a multiplicity of actualizing entities, a multiplicity, that as actual*ized*, is more or less included in each occasion as a non-personal society composed of the then most recent actualizations of many personal strands.

So the question of necessary existence comes down to whether or not a society exists that has no first member, has a present member and must always have new members. All members, all actual entities are contingent, but it does not follow that all societies must exist contingently. The dipolar answer will be that since each non-fragmentary Actual Entity of a necessarily existing personal society depends on inheriting a non-personal society composed of fragmentary creations as its subordinate pole, if all the personal strands composing the non-personal societies were to die, not only would the non-personal societies not exist, any personal society (including the proposed divine society) that depended on them would also cease. So, can one make sense of a society composed of perspectival actual occasions that must exist?

Each cosmic epoch will likely have its own Chain of Being, composed of nexūs of actual entities similar to the four groups noted by Whitehead above, but every possible cosmological set of species must have a lowest-level society upon which higher order species depend and build. Each member of this lowest-level, non-personal society will exhibit a bare minimum of creative ability: Each member will be nearly indistinguishable from another. A member of such a society will exhibit metaphysical conditions, as must all actual entities, but it will have a minimum of contingent embellishments.

This minimally complex society cannot die since nothing disrupting enough can occur that would prevent it from perpetuating new members. Imagining this society is really an exercise in intellectual abstraction, myth-building, if you will, since not only has there has always been minimally creative actual entities (no matter how far back one wants to imagine); but it is likely there have always been complex personally ordered societies, even though no particular mid-level society has always existed nor will continue to exist forever, since all were created contingently and will only survive so long as favorable contingent, environmental conditions continue.

Since nothing exists except dipolar actual entities, a discussion of either a necessarily existing personal society (composed of non-fragmentary actual entities) or of a necessarily existing non-personal society (composed of fragmentary actual occasions of minimal complexity) alone is incomplete and would likely commit the Fallacy of Misplaced Concreteness.

Seeing how the Categories are exhibited by actual entities of the lowest-level, non-personal society (which is also the unavoidable subordinate pole of the cosmic, personal society) will allow a discussion of the anatomy of an actual entity without becoming too bogged down in the contingent factors actual entities may exhibit. The inclusive pole composed of *non-fragmental* Actual Entities, will be discussed further in the next chapter.

THE UNAVOIDABLE SUBORDINATE POLE

The Category of the Ultimate expressed as, "Each of many wholes that comes to be is a part in many successive wholes," makes clear that the ultimate form of reality is social: Every actual entity is just one moment in a social nexus. Two societies stand out as necessarily existing, that is, having no first members nor having possible last members. These societies require some of their members to be sequentially ordered and others to exist as mutual contemporaries.

The primary implication, then, of the Category of the Ultimate, is that something or other must exist: "Nothingness" is not conceivable. The "transition" side of the Category expresses the necessity that something must exist even though every actual entity perishes: A new dipolar actuality must occur at the satisfied terminus of a process to accept its determination and thereby maintain the society. An actual entity can only come to be, can only reach a satisfaction, by being a datum (the privileged datum) for a new actual entity. Each member of the lowest-level non-personal society must not only be a datum for a successor as it reaches a satisfaction, but each member will reach a satisfaction because nothing exists to prevent it. Even if enough chaos could be generated to prevent some from reaching their satisfactions, some would still necessarily reach a satisfied state by conditioning new occasions in the society.

Further, if a cosmically inclusive Person is the most satisfactory way to rationalize the meaning of "the past" and "cosmic unity," this Person could not exist without a world to provide new data to include and surpass as each of its dipolar moments begins.

A minimally creative occasion, M, must not only reach a satisfaction, that is, not only must it be the immediate and primary (privileged) datum for a new occasion, N, it will always be only one of several data sources for the new occasion, N. Other occasions whose process durations started before M's transition to N will be contemporary processes of N; they will be sustaining the beings that were their initial data. Those processes whose initiating beings are also contiguous to N as it begins will provide additional data for it.

A minimally creative actual entity is still one with *some* creativity; some finite quantum of creativity is necessary. The attempt to cool atoms to "absolute zero" is impossible; it would be actuality with no process, no creativity; it would be "nothingness." There must be some heat, some creative energy, or nothing would exist to be cold. There must be the creating of something new. The necessary uniqueness of the initial data that multiple inheritances provide, establishes the unique potency, the subjective aim, for each actual entity.

Creating something novel is not making actual something that is fully specified (yet still remains a potential). Each actual entity begins with a unique database. The "mental" processing whole brings into existence a feeling never felt just like it before, however, it doesn't bring a new feeling into existence from "nothing." Even divine creative power must start with prior creations. The new feeling is always more or less like old feelings.

The minimally creative occasion develops new feelings nearly identical to those of its inherited causal past. Whitehead overstates the case a bit when he says "inorganic entities are vehicles for receiving, for storing in a napkin, and for restoring without loss or gain" (*PR* 177). To be "new"

The Necessarily Existing Society of Perspectival Occasions

requires a comparison to what is not new. The "old" is previous accomplishments relative to the standpoint of the new-making actual entity. Since comparison is always a simultaneous feeling of a contrast, the old must be present as a part of the present to contrast with the present whole and other parts in the whole.

Each actual entity in the other necessary society, the unsurpassable personal Society, is unsurpassed in the amount of data it begins with each moment (namely, all the beings ever created as it begins), and is unsurpassed in the quality of its new creation.

No moment can alter in any degree the datum with which it began. The past is and must remain forever as it is, or "the past" has no logical reference. Since the datum is the potentiality for the processing actual entity, it is the carrier of the universal, objective aim as well as the moment's specific aim, the actual entity's total datum complex. The initial aim remains constant throughout the moment's duration because it is an aim at a continuum of possibility; it is a somewhat generic direction. The processing actual entity specifies further the initial aim but does not change the fact that the initial aim was and remains just the generic potency it was. Process *adds* specificity but does not alter the initial conditions of the past that founds the new present subject.

The initial data, which particularize the completely generic, objective aim, are always vectored, coming from somewhere into the present. Those vectors "suggest" where the termination of the moment will be, barring any creative effort of the present whole to alter them. Altering the vectors requires an effort likely beyond the creative ability of minimally creative occasions. Actual occasions of minimal creative ability likely lie in the regions of "empty space" in our cosmic epoch. These occasions transmit feelings with little alteration of quality, direction and significance.

The Unsurpassable's moments can influence the vectors of fragmentary occasions forming contingently existing personal societies, but spatial movement of the unsurpassable Person is meaningless since that nexus is always everywhere simultaneously.

If the mentality of the moment cannot create a new quality of feeling, it can still create something new by adjusting the intensity or importance of the datum's qualities for those who inherit its satisfied superject. Such adjusting does not alter the datum. It overlays the past with new feeling so that as a whole the past, or some aspect of it, is felt more or less intensely. Such created changes to the values of the datum in an actual entity is one thing every process does. "Concrescence" cannot mean the "growing together" of parts not together at the initiation of the moment. All inherited parts exist together simultaneously as one complex datum. Those that have been created at the same time relative to the present moment are inherited coordinately.

> Thus, an act of experience has an objective scheme of extensive order by reason of the double fact that its own perspective standpoint has extensive content, and that the other *actual entities are objectified with the retention of their extensive relationships.* These extensive relationships are more fundamental than their more special spatial and temporal relationships (*PR* 67, emphasis added).

Any beings that are not newly created are parts of those that are. Beings that are mediated or ordered successively are nested deeper the older they are, thereby exhibiting the extension of temporal order. Temporal order exhibits successive differences. For "change" to be meaningful, there must be successive differences of the "same thing," and the differences, though successive, must be felt together, simultaneously contrasted, within the same subject whole. The "same thing" is the temporally extended event composed of more than one actual entity where each new actual entity includes the result of the previous actual entity, in what Whitehead calls "personal order." The dipolar present contains the immediate past and the more distant past as mediated or embedded in the immediate past. Thus the immediate past and the more distant past can both be simultaneously compared in the present.

There is a limit to how much the significance of the past can be increased or decreased within one actuality, but once decreased, novelty for future moments can be found in an increase and vice versa. Such changes in significance lie at the base of rhythm and likely the wave nature of spatial-temporally extended events that is most noticeable in contingently existing low-level societies. These societies are more or less personally and nonpersonally ordered.

Occasions at the very bottom of the creative hierarchy, those of minimal spatial inclusiveness and creative inventiveness, some of which must always be existing, are, as all actual entities, members of personally ordered strands. This follows from the necessity for every successful actual entity, M, to end as the beginning of a new actual entity, N. This does not exclude other beings from necessarily being included in N as parts of N's initial data, but these others are determinations made somewhat earlier than N's initiation by M's superject, the "privileged" datum for N. These others are maintained by other processes contemporaneous with N whose being-parts are contiguous to N as N is founded.

In the lowest-level society, the difference between the initial datum the privileged actual entity inherits and other contiguous data it must include is insignificant. In the lowest-level society, no temporal nexus has achieved a measure of complexity beyond that of the average of the others in the society.

Every being must be a datum in some dipolar actual entity or other: Beings are the "bodies" of creating wholes. "Personal order" becomes significant only when the bodies of a personal society are less complex than the privileged actual entities that form the personal society. No such mid-level personal society is necessary. How they come to be is a topic for cosmology, not metaphysics. How they die is a topic for metaphysics only because some metaphysical formulations seem to deny mid-level personal societies can die.

VALUE THEORY

The range of possible outcomes for an actual entity always contains some that are co-equally good and some that are not. At the lowest level of creative activity, the is-ought dimension is insignificant. There is too little room for entertaining alternatives. What will occur is not (significantly) different from what ought to occur. The same collapse of the is-ought dimension occurs at the highest or unsurpassable level of personally ordered Actual Entities, that is, each moment's creation by the most recent cosmic Whole's creation is as good as any other possible, not, however, because divinity created it, but because the Unsurpassable cannot act in ways that are surpassable by another. Of course, the next Whole of the unsurpassable society, not only will, but must surpass the Society's prior Whole by including it as a part of the present unsurpassed Whole. *Every* actual entity's accomplishment is surpassable, but only one each moment is can be unsurpassed. "Unsurpassability" can only be an attribute of a society: It can't be an attribute of any moment, of any state of affairs: Only the always all-inclusive, personal Nexus is unsurpass*able*. The seeming circularity of this argument will only evaporate if the definition of "unsurpassable" makes sense and does so in a modally necessary way.

For occasions forming personal societies that reach a level of complexity capable of supporting consciousness, choice between different possible outcomes becomes meaningful. Such moral choices (for better or worse) are made on what one believes to be the meaning of "good." Even if one knew what the meaning of "good" is (that is, the "objective aim"), and wanted to do something as good as possible, how one ought to fulfill one's subjective aim, is not always obvious since knowledge of the total context is impossible. For this reason many argue that since one always acts in light of what one sees as good, all "evil" is the result of ignorance, that is, evil is the result of tragedy, namely, the loss of valuable future outcomes due to a confluence of circumstances no one chose.

Chapter 7

The Necessarily Existing Society of Non-Perspectival Occasions
Maximally Creative Processes

> There is the vague sense of many which are one; and of one which includes the many. . . . There are two senses of the one—namely, the sense of the one which is all, and the sense of the one among the many (*MT* 110).

> At least two basic forms of contrast are not abolished by metaphysical conceptions. One is that between God and any other individual being; the other is that between logical types . . . a metaphysician must eschew extreme nominalism, he must admit that distinctions of logical type have counterparts in extra-linguistic reality . . . Metaphysics by definition takes necessity to be ontological as well as logical . . . In addition to the most general or neutral idea of reality, spanning all logical types, we need metaphysical universals valid only within one type . . . For where there are no definite common aspects there are no definite contrasts either (*CSPM* 138–142).

EVERY ACTUAL ENTITY MUST embody all the metaphysical principles that define what all actual entities are, namely, how all actual entities are necessarily the same, that is, exemplifying the Category of the Ultimate and all the Epochal Categories. Whitehead sets this as the goal of metaphysical speculation: "The metaphysical characteristics of an actual entity—in the proper general sense of 'metaphysics'—should be those which apply to all actual entities" (*PR* 90).

> The presumption that there is only one genus of actual entities constitutes an ideal of cosmological theory to which the philosophy of organism endeavours to conform. The description of the generic character of an actual entity should include God, as well as the lowliest actual occasion, though there is a specific difference between the nature of God and that of any occasion (*PR* 110).

Yet, every actual entity does and must differ from all others in some ways because the actual world from which it arises is unique, and what it does with its inheritance is unique. That every actual entity is unique is one of the universal necessities that all actual entities have in common. The way all actual entities must be alike are metaphysical characteristics. How they differ depends on the created contingencies unique to each moment.

This contrast between abstract necessities all actual entities have in common and the concrete differences each one exhibits, is often left as the whole truth. However, there are differences amongst actual entities that are not just factual differences, but are necessary differences. Whitehead seems to call a difference of this type a "specific difference" (*PR* 110), but he is not clear that this difference, this contrast, is, as Aristotle would say, an apodictic or modal difference, a contrast of logical types.

The necessary differences are modal contrasts, which means one actual entity is necessarily supreme or unsurpassed during each present moment, while all others are necessarily surpassed. What makes an actual entity supreme is not that it necessarily exists in all ways just as it does as opposed to others who exist as they do contingently. *All* actual entities exist as they do contingently; this follows from the necessity for every actual entity to inherit contingently created data and (for every successful actual entity) to create a contingent result as it perishes as a datum for others. Even though an actual entity exists necessarily forever as a determinate being in others, "objectively immortal," still it came into existence at some time so it hasn't always existed, therefore, it obviously didn't have to exist, unless "complete determinism" makes sense.

If Whitehead says (and I don't find it completely clear that he does) that God is one actual entity and the only one existing necessarily (contrary to all other surviving realities that must be societies of actual entities), this would seem to make God's "specific" difference so unique that the generic characteristics all actual entities have in common could not apply to God/

The Necessarily Existing Society of Non-Perspectival Occasions

dess. The Epochal Categories suggested here for defining what every actual entity has in common do apply to those of the divine personal society without exception and without equivocation. However, there are Categories that necessarily distinguish God/dess from any other actual entity or society of actual entities.

All necessities are abstract and changeless, but there are necessities, the Modal necessities, that express a necessary dipolar contrast between one class (species) of actual entities and another, namely, those that are necessarily unsurpassed in quantitative inclusion and qualitative value when they occur, and those that are necessarily surpassed.

That said, necessities must be grounded in actuality, for as Hartshorne says, "Metaphysics by definition takes necessity to be ontological as well as logical . . ." (*CSPM* 138). Nothing exists but actual entities, and all are contingent, so what can exist necessarily to maintain the necessities that metaphysicians seek? I have attempted to discuss the Categories as much as possible one group at a time. But the discussion of the Epochal Categories, which focused on minimally creative actual occasions so as not to bring in contingently created embellishments, still had to discuss a non-personal social group of low-level actual occasions as well as the ubiquitous actual entities of the cosmic personal Society. Here again, clarifying "necessary existence" as a modal difference from "contingent existence" must draw on the societal organization of actual entities rather than the alteration and perpetration of just one actuality. Such an alteration of a single reality would be a return to the substance-attribute metaphysics.

"Necessary existence" is a social attribute of actual entities. What necessarily exists is not a necessary actual entity or group of them, but "some *contingent* actual entity or other" at every moment of the social nexus. In addition to the necessity for there to be a lowest-level, non-personal society there must be a necessarily existing Society at the highest level, a personal society composed of Actual Entities, as are all societies, each of which is unsurpassed when it occurs, and when it is surpassed, it must be by the next member of the unsurpassable personal Society itself. The next member of the Society includes it as its privileged datum along with all other new determinations the world has just created.

Being unsurpassed at each present moment is the only way to assure that there will always be some contingent actual entity *or other* in the personal Society, the meaning of "necessary existence." The personal *society* of

75

unsurpassed Actual Entities is not just unsurpassed (as is each moment of the Society when it occurs); it is unsurpass*able*.

Hartshorne greatly helped to clarify this issue with his trichotomy of What, That and How: The definition is *what* one is referring to (its "essence"); *that* refers to something existing exemplifying that definition, and *how* describes the way the existence is concretely fulfilled each moment. In the case of a "necessarily existing reality," *that* it must exist is part of *what* it means (*AD* x–xii). So if one can make sense of *what* it means, s/he has established *that* it must exist. One need not know *how* something existing necessarily is existing as long as one can know *that* the something (a personal social nexus) is existing in some contingent way or other. So long as there is *some how or other*, it exists, and in this unique case there must be some how or other, *if* "necessary existence" makes sense.

So, again, one need not, and should not, try to define a "necessarily existing actual entity" or "being." It would be a major exception to the meaning of an "actuality," all of which are contingent in how they exist: No particular actuality must occur. "Necessary existence" is not an attribute of any actual entity: All are contingent. What is necessary is the necessity for the greatest conceivable personal Society to always be creating some contingent (though at that moment, unsurpassed) Being or other.

Anselm (1033–1109), after some stumbling around in *Proslogium* II, finally pointed out correctly in *Proslogium* III that the modally superior form of existence is "necessary existence." Given two existing realities, one that must exist and one that need not exist, the one that one that exists without any possibility of not existing surpasses the one that might fail. "Necessary existence" must surpass "contingent existence" *but only if* "something existing necessarily" makes sense. Anselm believed it did make sense as "God," but Anselm thought "God" was a necessary being, a changeless being, an act so complete it could not ever be added to or altered: an actuality that doesn't act. But all concrete realities are contingent; any one could have been otherwise or not at all. All necessities, on the other hand, are changeless, and all changeless characteristics are abstract; yet for something to exist, it must be concrete; it must act. Anselm was willing to make the existence of God such an exception to what "existence" means that it failed to convey any meaning (as Positivists have long pointed out); it stands as a major incoherence in his classical theistic worldview.

Anselm's valuable insight was not that "necessary existence" makes sense, but that atheism, agnosticism and empirically based theism miss the modal point because all three assume that "God" makes sense as a contingently existing reality rather than a modally unavoidable reality. This is so because all three assume one can know *what* is referred to when discussing "God" without knowing *that* "God" exists. This ignorance is only possible if what one is referencing does not have to exist. Every contingently existing actuality will be surpassed by another, and every contingently existing society of actualities will be surpassed by a society that began before the contingent one came into existence and/or will continue after it ceases. A society that must always exist would be existing before and after any other society, *if* a "necessarily existing reality" makes sense. We can excuse Anselm for jumping too quickly to the assumption that it does make sense, but it is hard to excuse present-day thinkers for assuming the Theistic Arguments still depend on Classical Theism's attempted definition of "necessary existence."

Part of the definition of "unsurpassable existence" is to exist necessarily. Hartshorne calls this the Anselmian Principle: Necessary existence surpasses, *necessarily* surpasses, contingent existence. Even though "existence" must be a metaphysically generic characteristic that must unequivocally mean the same thing for everything that exists to avoid systematic incoherence, namely, "something that is doing something," an actuality, an act, still the possibility of a meaningful modal difference amongst existences must be considered. By distinguishing the particular states of existence a personal society *may* have from the necessity that the society *must* have some states or other in order to necessarily exist, the equivocation on what "endurance through time," that is, what "endurance through changes," means can be eliminated. "Endurance through changes" always means a "succession of actual entities in a social nexus," a personal society, never the continuance of one altering actual entity: Every actuality acts only once.

A "personal society" is a unique succession of actual entities wherein each actualized entity of the series is inherited by one privileged actual entity that begins with the successful termination of the prior's act. (The superjects of other additional actualized entities must also be inherited.) In this way every actual entity can be concrete and contingent without assuming that every personal society must exist contingently. The question can then be asked: Is there a personal society that necessarily exists, that is, one that could not have a first moment or a last moment? This question is the same as asking: Does such a society make sense? Making sense is the only relevant proof. Empirical evidence is necessarily neutral on the issue.

The usual retort to this proposal is that a personal society requiring new contingent states cannot be complete or perfect and, therefore, is or would be surpassed by a reality that was so complete there would be no need to have new states since all possible states are eternally fulfilled. However, the belief that "all possible states actualized" has a coherent meaning is the mistaken assumption of Classical Theism. Every state has value, but possible states of value are endless, and there are always those that are incompatible together. Every state of value is a selection or creation of a state of value that is incompatible with other possible states at that moment. Only by fulfilling states of value sequentially can those states not possible together at one moment become possible. "The greatest possible state of value," is only meaningful if it means, "the unsurpassed state of value now," but it cannot be meaningful as "all values timelessly fulfilled."

In short, what "God/dess" means, what historically has been the divine "essence," should not be simply contrasted to "existence." Something can exist in many ways. Each particular way is an act, *how* the essence is actualized. Every actuality is contingent, but that does not settle the question of the modal status of what exists. Something exists so long as it is acting in some way or other. If part of the definition or essence of God/dess is a reality that must exist, then *what* one is referring to and knowing *that* it exists are one and the same, *if*, that is, "necessary existence" makes sense. That it does is no easy task to establish, but as Hartshorne says,

> So long as philosophers persist in confusing existence and actuality, just so long will they be but bumbling amateurs in a matter in which they have long been claiming competence (*AD* xi).

ALL-INCLUSIVENESS

To exist necessarily is only one characteristic an unsurpassable mode of existence requires to be meaningful. The reality that is unsurpass*able* in value is the personal Society that must have all possible values, that is, all past states and all future states (as its dipolar subordinate pole) when they become actualized. This reality exists unsurpassed at each moment. To meaningfully be an "unsurpassed actual entity" it must be superior to all others in quantity and quality, in size and value. In addition, it must always have a time designation since there is no timeless state of value that can't and won't be surpassed. Every state must be surpassed by the present

The Necessarily Existing Society of Non-Perspectival Occasions

unsurpassed state. Every actual entity is surpass*able*, including what the Unsurpassable just created, but one and only one act in the present can be necessarily unsurpass*ed*, and it is simply the present creative process of the unsurpassable personal Society.

All actual entities include the actualizations of others. To be assured that an actual entity is unsurpassed in inclusiveness, it must include every actualized entity. It must be contiguous to, overlap or include, every being brought into being up to that time. At every transition to a new all-inclusive actual entity, three classes of beings exist: (1) There is the just-created Being that the immediately prior all-inclusive actual entity came to be and has flowed into the next "privileged" actual entity of the cosmic Person as its privileged datum; (2) there are all the beings just created by actual entities that are not all-inclusive, because they had to take a perspective on the universe since they could not be contiguous to every previous creation; and (3) there are all the beings that have come to be in the past that are present in the present because they are contained within, that is, mediated by, those that succeeded them that are immediately in the cosmically inclusive coming-to-be.

So long as the members of the Series of all-inclusive comings-to-be occur more rapidly than any fragmentary actual entity can occur, there will be no chance that a being could exist that is not included. Reality is a multiplicity of actual entities in process as contemporaries. There will always be fragmentary actual occasions in process as contemporaries of each all-inclusive Process. This is why the One is always "one amongst many" actual entities. Though the prior all-inclusive member of the unsurpassable personal Series is immediately part of the datum for the new all-inclusive process Whole as it reaches its satisfaction, there will be actual occasions that terminate just before the new Whole begins. Each of these occasions had to terminate as a datum for a successive, privileged perspectival occasion according to the Category of the Ultimate. Therefore, since every *successful* actual entity initiates another actual entity, every being that has come to be is immediately part of a new process. "[T]he subjective forms of the immediate past are continuous with those of the present" (*AI* 183).

Whether or not the new process, N, succeeds in creating a new being, the old, inherited being it contains is available to be prehended by other contiguous nascent actual entities, as long as N lasts, and will always be prehended by the next all-inclusive, non-perspectival Whole. This is the sense in which the One is not one amongst many, but a One inclusive of the

Process and Dipolar Reality

many. As process, the universe is irreducibly a multiplicity, but as determinate beings, the universe is gathered up into a process One, a new One each moment that includes the old One as a determinate Being and the complete past it mediates, plus all other newly determined beings and the pasts they mediate.

RELATIVITY AND COSMIC SIMULTANEITY

An unsurpassed actual entity is not only a Whole that includes all that has come to be prior to its initiation, but as a satisfied superject it is an unsurpassed cause in others. Every unsurpassed Actual Entity begins with the last Being created as its privileged part; every fragmentary being begins just after the latest Being has come to be. It will be contiguous to that Being and must include it as a datum. Since it is not obvious that non-divine actual occasions include the whole universe and its past, even those who find that prehending God/dess' determinate creations makes sense will likely maintain that most of the divine Being is 'negatively" prehended by fragmentary actual occasions. I must hold that all of the most recent Being is prehended by every actual entity, for the following reasons:

First of all, the determinate Being has a unity; it comes as one datum. It is one amongst the many beings that are found at the foundation of every actual entity. Secondly, being is potentiality, and potentiality is a continuum with no way to cut off some and leave the rest. Most of each cosmic Being will shade off into irrelevance, but "complete irrelevance" is impossible. A being just created that is sustained by an occasion not contiguous to the nascent occasion under consideration here, will not be included in, nor be potentiality for, that occasion. This is the basis of contemporaneousness and causal independence of occasions, but a being prehended is the whole being prehended. Even though most of it may be causally insignificant, none of it has zero affect.

This is where I hold that Whitehead is right on: Every being—*all* of every being—is a potential for *every* actual entity, given two qualifications: (1) No being can be a potential for actual entities already in process or satisfied, and (2) a fragmentary being, though included in a cosmic process (but not yet a part in a superjective cosmic Being), will only be a potential for (a) the next fragmentary actual occasion that follows as a privileged occasion, along with (b) others that occur contiguous to that being. However, once it is objectified as part of the cosmic Actual Entity's satisfied/superject, it

The Necessarily Existing Society of Non-Perspectival Occasions

will be prehended and be part of the potency of every new actual entity, no matter how distant, forever.

Every being is *one* potential, one continuum. Even when many potentials are prehended together simultaneously as an actual entity is established, all-together they provide one complex potential for the actual entity, that is, its datum, felt as its subjective aim. The objective aim is the universal aim or purpose of existence that has been from the infinite, primordial past an objective part of every actual entity, as is every metaphysical principle. The complete past is contained in the latest divine Being; this Being, along with all other beings prehended as an actual entity begins its life, particularize the objective, universal aim and give the actual entity a unique subjective aim, a continuum of potentiality always directed, however vaguely, by the unavoidable metaphysical aim.

Since the divine epochal durations, that is, the cosmic Nexus' temporal comings-to-be, are as quick as any other, and since each cosmic Actual Entity is related to all actual occasions of the world first by including their creations and then by conditioning all new comings-to be, every occasion (with the two noted exceptions above) is influencing others everywhere in the universe as mediated by the divine series, and is, therefore, influenced by creations from everywhere regardless of distance. This metaphysical Theory of Relativity seems to be in conflict with the accepted understanding of the physical Theory of Relativity that maintains influence can only be transmitted at a finite rate, probably the speed of light. Note, first of all, that even in the metaphysical theory presented here, transmission or mediated influence can only occur at a finite rate, namely, the finite temporal extension that a divine process takes to create a new Being. Admittedly, this must be very fast, so the concern for the nearly instantaneous influence across the universe is valid. This comic relativity should be easier to accept, however, now that the "collapse" of an entanglement has proven to be instantaneous regardless of the spatial separation of the entangled members.

The usual alternative to a universe that is a *uni*verse because of a cosmic, simultaneous prehension of all that exists (as determinate) each moment, is to maintain the unity of the universe is one Space, a theory adopted even by Einstein that goes back at least to Democritus. It has serious logical problems having to do with the relations of the one and the many, parts and whole, unity and diversity, and so on. As attempts are made to unify the physical Theory of Relativity and Quantum Mechanics, space is looking much less like one "thing," and more like a multiplicity of occasions, leaving the question of cosmic unity unanswered, if even addressed.[9]

The only reason a series of cosmic fronts or durations seems incompatible with Relativity theory, is the unwarranted assumption that cosmically mediated influence throughout the universe would be obviously detectible. All measuring instruments are made of atoms and molecules, usually large groups of them. A physical measurement detects an average that ignores individual actions. Individual physical entities like protons and electrons are composed of lengthy personal societies embedded in numerous fields. We know little about their subtleties. The ubiquitous cosmic influence is less about unique influence than about the constant background against which the uniqueness of more localized beings exert their more obvious causal power due to their proximity. To be as concerned with the interior of distant stars as a truck bears down on one crossing a street would be a very negative evolutionary adaptation. The physical Theory of Relativity's denial of cosmic simultaneity seems true only because it deals with massive objects. It is "true," but at a high level of abstraction. One must be very dogmatic to assert it denies the possibility of cosmic simultaneity, and of a completely non-local prehensive ability and influence.

The unsurpassable Reality requires "dual transcendence" as Hartshorne points out. To be defined as "unsurpassed" requires being unsurpassed in any way logically possible, and to be unsurpassed in both passivity and influence, that is, being unsurpassed in the number of others influenced and the number of others being influenced each moment, seems logically meaningful. It is really another way to acknowledge the ultimate dipolarity of reality: *a subject of all objects that comes to be an object for all new subjects*. This is the unsurpassed fulfillment of the Category of the Ultimate at each moment that only the Unsurpassable Nexus can unsurpassably achieve.

UNSURPASSABLE QUALITY

Plato (as Socrates) asked whether something is "loved because it is holy . . . [or] holy because it is loved" by the gods (*Euthyphro* 10): Is something good because God/dess does it, or does God/dess do it because it's good. Similarly, are metaphysical principles necessary because God/dess makes

---

9. Perhaps some will argue that the Higgs' field will step in to answer the question of cosmic unity.

them so, or are they necessary because there is no conceivable alternative to them? Any significant discussion of theism comes down to this modal issue: Is God/dess the unsurpassable exemplification of the unavoidable principles of existence, or did God/dess establish them as one set of principles out of other possibilities? If the latter, the "concept" of unsurpassed goodness seems meaningless. "Supreme goodness" collapses into "supreme power," a concept often attempted to mean "all power," which fails to be a coherent notion unless it means "some power everywhere." For an actual entity to exist at all it must have some processing power; a reality with "all the power" would have nothing to influence or have power in.

Attempts to venerate "God" by exempting "God" from the necessary concepts defining what it means to be something, fail by making "God" unintelligible. But actual entities can vary in the amount of concrete content they embrace and in the quality of their creations. Each moment there can only be one Actual Entity that is supremely inclusive and supremely valuable. Because quality of value resides partly in the amount of value included, one must be all-inclusive to be unsurpassed in value. But even given the same amount of inclusiveness, actual entities can vary on the value or quality of their creations. The highest level of value is that which is unsurpassed at the moment. Since there are co-equal possible values, even an actual entity in the divine Nexus that creates an unsurpassed satisfaction, could have done something else and still be unsurpassed. All differences are not differences of better or worse.

However, since every actual entity must arise from a particular situation and create a result that cannot include all possibilities and their values as actualized, every creation, even if unsurpassed at the time, is capable of being surpassed by adding new value to what has already been accomplished. "Unsurpassability" cannot be an attribute of any state of affairs, but it can be an attribute of a personal series. If a person must exist whose moments must be unsurpassed when they occur, and if only this person can surpass the prior moment by including it and adding to it, then this person would be unsurpassable by any other actual entity or personal series. The Unsurpassable Series not only can, but must, surpass what was actualized in the past since there are innumerable possible states of value yet to be actualized. If the Unsurpassable didn't continue forever surpassing the past by adding new values, someone else could be conceived to do so and this personal nexus would necessarily surpass the so-called unsurpassable series, because a series that does not add new value each moment is dead.

Determining whether or not such a personal series exists is not an empirical exercise; it is an examination of modal concepts. Any concept that makes sense as unsurpassable must be an attribute of the Unsurpassable Personal Series. Concepts that make sense as "supreme" are attributes of a created state of affairs at a certain date. Concepts that are meaningful without qualification, without reference to when something occurs, are "ultimate." An ultimate attribute can only apply to a personal society, never to one moment, no matter how complete or rich in value it is. All ultimate characteristics of reality are metaphysical: They are changeless and timeless aspects of reality. The argument put forth here is that only as attributes of a personal society of ever-new unsurpassed moments, as attributes of a primordial and everlasting Society, can the ultimate abstractions of metaphysics find a concrete, yet eternal home.

"Necessary existence" is an ultimate attribute. A reality "existing necessarily" surpasses any reality that exists contingently because a necessary existence must have always existed and could never cease existing. Any "thing" that survives changes and carries an identity through time cannot be one actual entity or one concrete state of affairs. It must be a personal society whose identity is maintained by a growing core of past feelings as it adds novelty at each moment. Even if a contingently existing person had no first moment (which is purely hypothetical since all contingent existences depend on others to initiate their existence), there is always the possibility that such a person will have a last moment. Not just the failure to exist at all, but the *possibility* of death is the real defect that is surpassed by a person whose existence is not conceivably in danger of ceasing. "Long-lasting" is a quantitative attribute which the Unsurpassable must exhibit; but the "impossibility of ceasing" is a qualitative difference of value from one who could conceivably cease.

LOVE

Because the word "love" has so many human psychological connotations, I hesitate to discuss it as a possible divine attribute. Yet, in a sufficiently attenuated sense, loving is a metaphysical necessity. Every whole is dipolar: The whole is the lover; the parts are the loved. Love always exhibits this two-sided dipolarity: embracing others as they are and desiring the best for those who must love what the lover creates. To exist lovingly is to embrace some data, an environment, while desiring to create a satisfaction that will

The Necessarily Existing Society of Non-Perspectival Occasions

enrich others' data. In a strict sense, an actual entity can never act for itself: It does enjoy or suffer others it inherits, and it does create new feelings, but it always perishes as a datum for others or gives up trying. Egoism is logically impossible except as it means "acting for the benefit of a narrow personal society." An unsurpassable Lover embraces all existing data and desires future others to be enriched.

In terms of "love," only a reality that cannot die can be unqualifiedly loved, or love others unqualifiedly. "I'll love you as long as you and I exist," is a different quality of love from "I have always loved you, and I always will." All other cases of professed unqualified love are hyperbole. Of course, one can only love unqualifiedly a reality that makes sense as necessarily existing (one can't love an impossible reality). No facts (all of which are contingent) are relevant to establish whether or not an unsurpassable lover makes sense. To make sense of a "necessarily existing reality" is not just to establish that it happens to exist, but rather that it must exist. One cannot establish that any particular state of affairs must exist since all states are contingent, but very cogent arguments can be marshaled to establish that some contingent whole or other must always be creating as the most recent member in the cosmic personal Nexus, and that the potentials for each all-inclusive member of that society must include all the ever-new beings created by occasions necessarily not all-inclusive.

The modal difference between a necessarily existing personal Series and contingently existing persons is not vitiated by the necessity that some non-personal society or other exists in addition to the divine personal Society. A lowest-level non-personal society must exist as the subordinate pole of each dipolar Whole, but any particular defining characteristic of such a non-personal society (that is, those in addition to the metaphysical characteristics) will eventually cease. It will be replaced by another since metaphysical dimensions alone cannot define the lowest-level, non-personal society, or any non-divine society. Each member will be objectively immortal, as is every actualized moment, but every mid-level, non-divine personal nexus has had a beginning and will end when the societies upon which it depends become too chaotic for the creative power it possess to bring about a new determination.

The difference between necessary and contingent existence is a modal difference of quality. The Whole must contain all that have come to be; others are able to contain only those contiguous to its initiation. The quality, then, of each Whole's inclusion of others is unsurpassed. Only the next moment of the Unsurpassable Series will surpass its previous Whole by adding new content. Each moment is surpassed unsurpassably. No reality could add more content nor add content with more aesthetic value. Others only include or love some others, and those each does include are felt with some vagueness, with an indistinctness denied to divinity except as the Unsurpassable feels with exact clarity the vagueness others feel.

Every member of every society has been or will be surpassed in some way by another present or future member. Only a society as a beginningless-and-endless series of acts can have the property of being "unsurpassable." Since non-personal societies never consist of occasions that can simultaneously include the results of *all* others, it is always possible to conceive of an occasion that includes more than any particular member does. Only a personal society can conceivably be composed of actual entities with the property of "all-inclusiveness." Non-personal societies always have members externally related to each other as contemporaries.

Only a personal Society can conceivably exhibit "unsurpassability" since it retains an identity through changes by addition of all that exists (including all its own past moments' accomplishments). No other society could conceivably surpass it because all others are necessarily parts of the moments of the all-inclusive personal Society. To be a personal society unqualifiedly unsurpassable, any attribute that that makes sense as an ultimate characteristic (those attributes descriptive of the society rather than its individual moments) must be a characteristic of the Unsurpassable Society.

Traditionally, attributes have been applied to divinity in two ways, either those qualities liked are said to be theistic attributes, such as, "loving," "knowledgeable," and "powerful," or God was described as "beyond loving," "beyond knowing," and so on. The *via negativa* denied any attribute was literally applicable to God, but even so, those attributes said to be possessed by God reflected a bias for one pole of a contrast not necessarily justified by their intrinsic meanings.

"Unsurpassability" is the inclusive defining characteristic of divinity as an Individual. It includes all other attributes literally that make sense as ultimate, that is, as applicable to the personal series with no temporal qualification. Qualifications are required for every other personal society. God/dess simply knows (all, clearly); others know some things unclearly.

In order to be unsurpassable, each moment of the Unsurpassable Individual must exhibit supremacy in all attributes that make sense as supreme. Attributes of supremacy always imply a date like "the biggest now" or "happiest now" or "most suffering now." Only someone who assumes that change is not possible could believe the "biggest now" or "the most beautiful now" could never be surpassed. When an unsurpassed "now" is surpassed, it must be accomplished by the next act of the Unsurpassable. It must be surpassed unsurpassably.

"Unsurpassable surpassing" is only logically possible if the next unsurpassed act includes (1) the prior unsurpassed actualization, otherwise it is conceivable that something could exist that does include that past actualization, and in doing so would be greater or more valuable than the act that didn't include it. The present act to be an unsurpassable surpassing of the prior unsurpassed Whole must also include (2) all new actualizations or, again, it would be conceivable that something could exist that would, and (3) all past accomplishments as mediated by more recent creations. Since what attributes are conceivable as ultimate or supreme is an issue of conceivability (not to be settled by facts or selected from a personal bias), even "negative" attributes must be considered.

Being "negative" implies a loss. The only losses possible are possibilities since all actualizations are saved. If they weren't, references to "the past" would be meaningless, and the so-called "Unsurpassable" could conceivably be surpassed. So all loss is loss of possible future situations. Every moment brings into being one of innumerable other possible states. These other possible states are unfulfilled or lost to the present moment, but only if a" better" state of affairs could have occurred are the losses negative. The future might still bring into actualization some aspects of those that did not occur. Only those situations that exemplify the ultimate standard of value less fully than they could have are more or less "bad" or negative.

Lost of future value can occur in two ways: deliberately or accidentally. Most situations are a mixture of the two. Insofar as blame can be assigned to deliberate loss, the act was evil. Non-deliberate loss is tragic; it's bad luck. Calling "acts of nature" that are destructive, or any accidental negative loss, an "act of God" is not just blasphemous, it's bad metaphysics. The failure to understand that the universe is necessarily populated with agents with some freedom and partial ignorance underlies many theological absurdities and psychological neuroses.

POSITIVE VALUE

Before considering whether God/dess must exhibit evil unsurpassably, what more might be said first about "unqualified goodness" or the "ultimate standard of value"? On the one hand, what is valuable is immediately felt by each moment embracing the actualized value. The conceptual analysis of that feeling of value discloses aesthetic categories, the most general of which is unified diversity, one side of the Category of the Ultimate: Nothing exists without some unity of contrasts, a unification somewhere between too much diversity and too much similarity, between chaos and bored-to-death.

Value is an intrinsic feeling each actual entity feels others have contributed to itself at its birth and a feeling it will contribute to others as it perishes successfully. However, in a world where not all values can be fulfilled, whose feeling of value is paramount? Whose value must ultimately be considered? If theism makes sense as a metaphysical necessity of reality, there is only one possible answer to the question: the Unsurpassable's feeling. All value is contextual; whether or not and how much any particular thing is valuable depends on how it fits in with all the rest. Ideally, it will enhance without diminishing others. But only an experience that feels *all* others can "judge" how it fits in with all others. Only a reality that knows or feels all the past and present actualizations and can foresee all there is to foresee about possible future outcomes can know how any particular creation fits in with everything.

Another consideration is longevity. To contribute value to something that will cease and nullify the contribution is, finally, to make no difference at all. No difference implies no value, whether good or bad. So once again, only a contribution to a reality that retains it all and cannot cease can be the measure of the value for what it is, forever. Logic dictates that the Unsurpassable is the only meaningful valuator of all values. Love as concern for how one's creations will alter the next Whole and all future Wholes, is the basis for a rational ethic.

Yet, because reality is dipolar, the way one changes the future of the Unsurpassable personal series is by changing oneself and, thereby, all the others that are contiguous to one's satisfaction. Perhaps with a slightly different meaning, the saying that insofar as you do something to the least of God/dess' creatures you do it to God/dess, is true because all are parts of the Whole. Giving to God/dess what is God/dess' and to Caesar what is Caesar's is bad theology since even Caesar is part of the divine Whole. So acting for God/dess without acting for others is impossible. Only by acting for others can one act for God/dess. The crux of the matter, however, is *how* one acts for others. "Others" always include those possible future actual entities in one's own personal society as well as those in other persons. How one acts, what one does, should be as enriching a fulfillment of the metaphysical purpose as possible.

HATE

Allied to love is hate, not by being love's opposite, but by being a neurotic and self-destructive form of love. Like love, hate is a desire, a desire to cause suffering for another personal society. Since one can only hate what one has embraced, hate can also be a desire to stop desiring anything to do with the hated person, that is, hate can be the desire to become indifferent to someone. Dwelling on the object of hate will only prolong the pain. Indifference is the true opposite of love, but complete indifference is only possible if one has never embraced the one towards which s/he is indifferent. Even if it were possible for worldly occasions to become indifferent to something once embraced, the unsurpassable personal Nexus cannot. Non-divine personal series can die, stopping the perpetuation of the pain and the desire to remove the pain. But the Unsurpassable has no option but to endure the pain. Knowing that whatever one does will remain forever an undoable part of reality is what gives life its poignancy.

Returning pain for pain, rather than preventing the person from causing future pain, will only make the Unsurpassable endure more pain forever. Only because one thinks a non-theistic metaphysics is meaningful, or one wherein only certain selected things are felt by God/dess, does revenge seem a rationally plausible idea. But if the "Unsurpassable" makes sense, "getting even" is metaphysically impossible. Reality is additive; one adds what enrichment one can, or one desires to be unlovable, an attribute somewhat possible only for non-divine persons. In reality, so long as one exists one must love some others and be somewhat lovable. Only death will stop one loving, stop one from embracing others. Not even death will stop what one has done from being embraced as part of reality forever.

The moral imperative is to create as loveable a state of affairs as possible as evaluated by the unsurpassable Evaluator, the only experience capable of considering the total context. The existential predicament we find ourselves in is not knowing for sure how cosmic reality will evaluate our acts. This divine judgment is not from a changeless eternity, but is renewed each moment as the many possibilities presented to each worldly and divine actualizing entity resolve into one determinate state of affairs. Though everything will be forever perpetrated, only what is enriching will be enhanced by future loving actual entities while the suffering of evil and tragedy will be minimized.

EVIL

Not only must all actual occasions alter the next dipolar Whole, but every Whole's satisfaction creates an environment with which the next duration of fragmentary occasions must begin. This all-pervasive environment will contain the cosmic past with aesthetic enhancements appropriate to all others in light of the primordial, objective aim. Each cosmic satisfaction will be as good as any other possible. Given that the cosmic Whole at each moment has to embrace all that had just come to be, it could not be surpassed in value. But why? Why isn't God/dess the "unsurpassable evil"? The Unsurpassable must experience the losses others create, that is, the Unsurpassable suffers, and does so unsurpassably. Of course, the Unsurpassable also experiences joy, more so than any other possible; but since evil is the deliberate loss of future enrichment, for evil to be an attribute of the Unsurpassable, the Unsurpassable would have to create a state so unenriching that no more loss would be possible. However, one can always conceive of a state a bit less enriched until the ultimate "state" of minimum value is "reached," namely, "nothingness." Since "nothingness" is not conceivable, the attempt to conceive of an "unsurpassable state of minimum value" is self-contradictory or meaningless.

If one attempted to conceive the "Unsurpassable" as only desiring the death or suffering of others, still every suffering that others experience must also be a pain for the Unsurpassable. Further, if all others, but God/dess, were to perish without initiating new actual occasions, a new Whole would not be possible since it would have no new parts to provide new potentiality for the Whole to fulfill. To abolish one side, the subordinate side, of the cosmic dipolarity, is to abolish the Whole also. "If you abolish the whole, you abolish its parts; and if you abolish any part, then *that* whole is abolished" (*PR* 288). So too, if you could abolish all potential parts, you would abolish all possible Wholes.

The Necessarily Existing Society of Non-Perspectival Occasions

The Unsurpassable cannot desire what is metaphysically impossible, namely, that reality cease. The Unsurpassable is only free to act in Unsurpassable ways, so just doing a bit of harm here and there is not theistically possible since more harm is always conceivable. The main point regarding negative attributes is that anything negative can only be conceived as localized or partial. Tragedy or evil can only partially disrupt a larger whole. When suffering becomes too much for a non-theistic whole to bear, it dies and its suffering ceases, so though some fragmentary wholes can be wiped out, nothing negative could eliminate all fragmentary wholes.

Further, no conceivable circumstances could prevent a theistic Whole from reaching a satisfaction. Each is the ultimate context for everything else. Each is supremely tolerant of any possible initial data, so if some of the world it inherits is painful, it will still reach a satisfaction that initiates the next nascent Whole. Negative feelings are only negative because they are retained. Overcoming evil with good does not involve the elimination of evil acts. Neither is evil or tragedy really a good *sub specie aeternitatis*. Neither is revenge a good response to an evil one suffers. It only creates more suffering. The only rational response to a negative situation is to do what one can to create new circumstances that minimize the negative feelings for all involved, and "all" includes the experience of One who cannot be insulated from feeling all feelings all others feel.

Pantheism is the antithesis of the social necessities embodied in the dipolar metaphysical Categories of panentheism. It is the ultimate solipsism; it implies that reality is either one whole that alters or a whole that does nothing.

Chapter 8

Necessary, Coordinate Contrasts within Process Wholes

ACTUAL ENTITIES

ACTUAL ENTITIES ARE THE most fundamental of units. Each is a dipolar unit, a whole with parts. Nothing exists unless it is either a part in a whole or is that which makes a whole more than its parts. The whole is always something in addition to its parts, but it's never something apart from its parts. The contrast between the whole and its inherited parts, a contrast contained within the whole, is the primary dipolar structure of reality. The kinds of contrasts that can be found in an actual entity exhibit the kinds of social relationships actual entities can or must have with each other.

To be very clear, contrasts within an actual entity are not of other actual entities, but of other actual*ized* entities. Creativity, that which is the subjectivity or wholeness of an actual entity, is never in another actual entity. Wholes are never parts: What a whole creates is a part for others. A subject creates, or comes to be, an object for other subjects. "The occasion arises from relevant objects, and perishes into the status of an object for other occasions" (*AI* 177). The whole does not create a determinate whole which then becomes a part in others. The determinate satisfaction a whole creates only exists as a part in other wholes. A whole, a subject, never experiences the determinate superject it creates. "No entity can be conscious of [or even prehend] its own satisfaction" (*PR* 85). The basic unity of an actual entity is its creative process, its "throbbing emotion," that "stands between its birth and its perishing" (*AI* 177).

CONTRASTS

An analysis of the inherited contrasts within an actual entity consists of the actual entity feeling the social ordering of the termini of other subjects, now objects, within itself. However, an actual entity must develop its own feelings. These feelings will contrast with its inherited feelings and with each other. An actual entity starts by feeling only the feelings others created, each with its own vector, but with one major difference: The many satisfactions inherited by an actual entity are felt as one complex coordinate contrast, the many felt simultaneously.

Further, each member's vector in the complete coordinate complex is contrasted with a general feeling of "direction," just generic enough to be the common denominator of all the individual, competing vectors. The subject's common "aim" is the urge to be new, to be different, always to be a specification within the universal, objective aim, the ultimate purpose, and a further specification of the novel, generic inheritance provided by the complex of beings that founds the subordinate pole of every dipolar actual entity.

Most contrasts an actual entity inherits are social structures that are not metaphysically necessary. They are the results of histories of creations that could have been otherwise. However, since one actual entity can only do one (complex) thing, and since its creation must begin with the termination of others, reality must consist of more than one actual entity. This means there must be both personal and non-personal societies: There must be a multiplicity of actual entities processing together. Some or all of their superjects prehended together as an actual entity's database form a non-personal society. What makes one society different from another is its history. A society has a contingent "defining characteristic" exhibited by each member of the society because each has inherited the same actualized entity or entities.

But "necessary," that is, unavoidable, defining characteristics, are also exhibited by every member of every society. These metaphysical dimensions have never been created, and cannot be used to distinguish one actual entity or society of actualized entities from another. They are not dateable, nor are they the result of an actual entity's creative activity. The most general or common factors of all facts are not facts; they are not "universals" that can be contrasted by their quality or location to other "universals" like colors, for example. Metaphysical principles are the only unqualified, eternal universals.

NECESSITIES IN THE CONTINGENT

A society is a nexus of actual entities that have inherited something in common. Since all actual entities inherit the same metaphysical dimensions, actual entities can't be "completely different" from each other. A world populated with actual occasions whose initial data have nothing contingently created in common is impossible because: (1) The received complex datum in every actual entity's initiation has a history that goes back indefinitely, likely infinitely, if complete forgetfulness is impossible. Something in that long history of the interactions of actual entities will be found in the initial data of all contemporary actual entities. (2) Each actual entity inherits the same cosmically omnipresent Being as part of its datum. This complex, coordinately related data prehended as one datum is process philosophy's reformulation of the "oneness of space." "Space" is not a single "material" thing, but the coordinate relationships of all prehended members of the most general society.

In this attempt to clarify the necessities actual entities exhibit as "the many," the radical coherence of the Categoreal Scheme becomes obvious: One cannot explain one aspect of the Scheme without assuming all others: If the "Unsurpassable" makes sense, it cannot do so as a contingent possibility to be brought in after clarifying how actual occasions must be ordered without considering the Unsurpassable. Since every actual entity must inherit the latest divine creation (because it is contiguous to all new actual entities), every actual entity is at least a member of a non-personal society defined by the last cosmic datum and all prior divine and non-divine actualizations as mediated by the most recent Whole's creation.

Since divine Beings are "universal" in the sense of being prehended everywhere there is anything, one might be tempted to say it is not a contingent defining characteristic because it is too much like the non-definite or non-limiting dimensions of the metaphysical scheme. But this is to ignore the necessity that every creation is what it is as opposed to an indefinite number of other possibilities. Even divine creations are contingent;

they are necessarily the most contingent because divine Wholes depend on everything being factors in what they come to be.

Dipolar reality requires there be subordinate factors or parts or there can be no whole. Each of the data parts included in a whole could have come to be differently from the way it did, and many, if not most, actual occasions could have failed to exist at all, namely, those whose complexity depends on less complex actualities. But this hierarchal dependency must end with the society of minimal complexity, the lowest-level, non-personal society that must exist just as surely as does the Unsurpassable Society. This is so because it is an essential, albeit subordinate, part of the dipolar Unsurpassable Society. But given the urge to novelty every occasion has, there have likely always been other mid-level non-personal and personal societies contingently developed by fragmentary occasions. So just as a *uni*verse cannot exist without a unifier of the many, a Whole with parts, neither can it exist without the multiverse of actual entities creating some new parts or other to be the subordinate pole of the cosmic dipolarity.

THE PAST AS COORDINATE STRUCTURE

The most straightforward approach to the unity of all that has just occurred is to have all the newly satisfied actual occasions be data for one all-inclusive nascent Actual Entity. These will be simultaneously prehended, that is, coordinately ordered *as given*. This will locate every occasion's determination relative to every other within that cosmic Whole. It is a spatial unity of objective parts within a Subject. But, again, unless a static, block universe makes sense, what came before the present and what will come after would not be parts in a Unifier that gathered up *just* the most recent fragmentary creations. Only by positing a Whole whose data also includes everything prior, is the past maintained as a logically meaningful object of reference and as something capable of being contrasted to the present. The reality of the totality of the fragmentary occasions' creations can only be rationalized if it exists somewhere and will be in existence forever.

The past, therefore, is not just the multiplicity of fragmentary occasions' creations. It's also their relationships; how they contrast with each other. "Concrescence" does not create these relationships. The way all determinations are related to each other at each moment in the past is more that just the individual determinations themselves. The reality of the past's simultaneous, that is, coordinate, relationships can only reside in past

Wholes that preserve these contrasts in the determinate Being each past Whole created. So, for the present Whole to really be all-inclusive of all the beings there are, it must also include all prior cosmically inclusive Beings. Every Being includes every prior Being. The Unsurpassable is unsurpassed because each moment includes all beings, present and past. If it were not all-inclusive of the past, it is conceivable that something else do so; and this something would surpass the so-called unsurpassed present. Since the future cannot be "in being," it cannot be included as actual. It will be included when it becomes created. To include the future as determinate being rather than generic potentiality, is to deny the future is any different from the past; or to claim omniscience does not know the difference.

Chapter 9

Necessary, Sequential Contrasts within Process Wholes

THE PAST AS SEQUENTIAL

To UNIFY THE UNIVERSE temporally as well as spatially, that is, sequentially as well as coordinately, there must be a personal Society all of whose members include the determinations of all prior members and whose future members not only will, but must, surpass unsurpassably their prior members' created Beings. Reality consists of many kinds of societies, but it always has had, and must always have, at least two kinds of societies in a dipolar relationship: An unsurpassable, personal Society whose subordinate pole must be at least a non-personal society composed of the complete multiplicity of all lowest-level personal strands. Each member of each society is dipolar: Each inherits the results of prior members of both societies. Neither society could exist without the other. The eternal metaphysical dimensions are only sustainable as changeless factors in a primordial and everlasting personal Society each of whose members is contingent, but a society that *must* have contingent members. This primordial and everlasting Society is the storehouse of all achievement; so all achievement does make a difference by influencing all future creations. "Any local agitation shakes the whole [future] universe" (*MT* 138).

The lowest-level society is the constant ground required for more adventuresome creations. It is the minimal source of novelty or impulse for all other actual entities, namely, other fragmentary neighbors and the next non-fragmentary Whole. Its creations are the inevitable body of the universe, food for all new momentary lives. As units of process, they are the irreducible multiplicity that is reality, amongst which even each Whole is "one among many." All societies, except the Unsurpassable and the lowest-level society, are both more complex than the lowest-level society and less complex than the Unsurpassable. Their very existences are not metaphysically assured.

Every intermediate-level society has come into being and will eventually cease supporting new members. All contingently existing societies are only more or less definable. What defines them is more like an emphasis on some items than an exact item or set of clear-cut characteristics. The Unsurpassable is categorically definable as *always* including *all* that has come to be. The lowest-level society is categorically definable as minimally complex and enriching, even though each member includes, with minimal significance, the totality of the universe as mediated by the last unsurpassed Being, and all its neighbors whose immediately prior creations are contiguous to it.

TRANSMISSION AND UNIVERSALS

To increase the complexity in the world, a member of the lowest-level society must create something "new." Logically speaking, every member of every society must do something somewhat new. Process must issue in novelty or it creates nothing at all. Everything created by members of the lowest-level society is radiated throughout the non-personal society: As each member comes to be, it extends the effect of the being it prehended a spatially finite distance farther from its originator. Given the lowest-level society where the only possible bodies that exist are contiguous others on the same level, every being created is immediately transmitted to others at the fastest possible (but necessarily) finite rate in all directions indiscriminately; even the transmission everywhere by way of divine mediation, as nearly instantaneous as it is, is still finite since each divine coming-to-be is temporally extended, so its superjects are not available until a new satisfaction exists.

Every satisfaction/superject, no matter how complex the particular is, begins its everlasting journey towards more universality as a factor in others, and will be found in more and more actual entities as new occasions occur wherein the past is mediated and becomes contiguous to, and data for, nascent actualities. But no such actualization-as-universal is ever truly "universal." Even if it could become a factor in all future actualities (as it does with some relevance as mediated by God/dess), it has not been a factor in all past actual entities. Such "universals" are not "eternal objects." Only the metaphysical characteristics are truly universal and eternal, that is, unavoidably exhibited by all actual entities. Though a "particular" (the unique datum created by an actual entity) becomes universalized, the eternal universals (the metaphysical Categories) become uniquely particularized in every actual entity.

Every non-eternal characteristic has been created at some time. Every qualitative "sense-datum" has been generated within the process of an actual entity; every quantitative pattern of qualities arises at a transition due to the simultaneous prehension of a multiplicity of beings, establishing the complex datum that forms the subordinate pole of the prehending actual entity. Within the lowest-level society, wherein there exists no specialized body to mediate and inhibit the immediate radiation of a satisfaction to other members of the society, the created factor radiates at a finite rate commensurate with its spatial-temporal volume (seemingly the ratio "c") that the members of the society have that are supporting the object.

TRANSMISSION VERSUS MOTION

Transmission should not be conceived as a being moving from one place to another. Every being created by an actual entity is a unique once-in-a-universe occurrence. It is what it is and where it is forever. There are prehensions of the one being from different standpoints which set up perspectives. In a personal series of actual entities, the "privileged" actual entity, the one that begins just as the prior member in its series reaches its determination, takes no perspective on the data created by the prior member of the series. The Unsurpassable, too, takes no perspective on its own past. Further, the unsurpassable personal Society is modally unique because it takes no perspective on any actual entity;[10] it is non-fragmentary, whereas the occasions

---

10. The popular expression is to maintain divinity has all the perspectives, but it is more accurate to simply say the cosmic Whole prehends all just as they are.

of all other personal societies must take a perspective on all others that are not their own pasts, including their unique perspectival prehensions of the ubiquitous cosmic Being. Perspective both leaves out all those that have just come to be that are not prior and immediately contiguous, and prehends non-privileged data, data being maintained by other personal societies, at an "angle" relative to the life-lines of these other societies.

A "life-line" is a personal society composed of actual entities wherein each begins with the prior moment's satisfaction; that is, a life-line is a series of actual entities each one of which begins with a uniquely created privileged datum. All other initial data that initiate a moment will be contiguous but will be held in existence by processes that began just before the process that started with the privileged datum.

Perspective arises because the spatial-temporal structure (or relationships of the parts of the datum) appears differently from each location within the structure, and because mediated data will have been modified before they are experienced. Even if the intensity of much of the mediated data were not downgraded before being prehended, it would be de-emphasized during the present creative process in order to keep and enhance those aspects of the initial data that are more relevant for personal survival. But there is nothing metaphysically necessary about this adaptation made by intermediate-level societies.

Chapter 10

Birth and Death of Hierarchal Relationships

IF THE METAPHYSICAL SCHEME offered here makes sense, two societies have always existed in a dipolar relationship: The unsurpassable, all-inclusive personal Society and the lowest-level non-personal society that is God/dess' secure body, albeit minimally inspiring. Since every actual occasion in this unavoidable, non-personal society must end as a determination that is immediately a datum for another occasion, this lowest-level non-personal society really consists of innumerable strands of personal order of minimum complexity.

> A nexus enjoys personal order when (α) it is a "society" and (β) when the genetic relatedness of its members orders the members "serially" (*PR* 34).

> A society may be more or less corpuscular, according to the relative importance of the defining characteristics of the various enduring objects compared to that of the defining characteristic of the whole corpuscular nexus (*PR* 35).

Apart from the ubiquitous comic creations, the only bodies occasions have in these personal strands are the beings other lowest-level occasions have created and maintain that are contiguous to each of the new occasions as they begin. So occasions in each personal strand are not somewhat insolated from their neighbors of the same minimal creative ability by a body, that is, the occasions in the lowest-level personal strands are not any more or less complex than any others in this society.

Every actual entity is somewhat unique, but to develop significant differences, the dumbing down of novelty by the environmental average, must be more or less avoided. This is the main function of a "body." The body of an actual occasion in a minimally complex society is whatever other minimally creative occasions have created. The bodies of occasions in the minimally complex society are no more complex than the environmental average because they are just the contiguous neighbors of the environment.

For a personal society to increase in complexity, it must be contiguous to a body more complex than the lowest-level society. The body must consist of societies more or less personal whose members (1) inherit from their prior and contiguous environment, including their own pasts, as do all actual entities, but also (2) inherit from the higher-level occasions in a personal society that depend on, but rise above, the bodily non-personal society of minimally creative personal strands by simultaneously prehending many members of the subordinate bodily society.

So between the all-inclusive, personal Society and the minimally creative non-personal society are, or may be, personal and non-personal societies of unimaginable variety, and endless new possibilities. As occasions become more complex, new patterns emerge. Tracing the rise of consciousness and the meaning of "truth" and "error," are contingent topics of interest. Laying the groundwork to comprehend perplexing physical phenomena like entanglement also arise within the contingency of created societies rather than exhibiting only metaphysical necessities, even though only an adequate and coherent metaphysic can give the ultimate context that allows one to fully understand what is happening contingently. The following topics of this chapter, are not metaphysically general, but illustrate some ways a process, event metaphysic can generate insights into some traditional philosophical topics.

BODIES

Every actual entity is a member of a personal society, from the occasions of minimal creativity to the unsurpassable, all-inclusive Person. Non-personal societies are always multiplicities of personal strands. A rock seems to be a multiplicity of personally ordered occasions that do not contribute simultaneously to a "rock" experience, so the non-personal society of the rock is not a body for a higher-level personal society. A "body" provides a multiplicity of personally ordered actual occasions, but occasions whose most recent satisfactions are simultaneously prehended by one, process whole. The data provided by the many for the prehender insures that its datum will be more complex than any one of the creations the non-personal bodily society provides.

The "central personal society" and the low-level personal societies that together comprise the body's non-personal society are in a constant give and take. Because the central or privileged person is more complex than any one of the actual entities in the non-personal society of the body, the datum it provides for its bodily members is more complex than the environmental average. It also provides a common influence for all the bodily occasions that tends to keep them sufficiently organized allowing them to return data to the privileged person. Their data will be more complex and more useful to maintain more complex future experiences than the occasions' superjects of the environment outside the body. But because the body is also contiguous to extra-bodily occasions as well as the occasions of the central person, the immediately contiguous environmental field will also be more complex than it would be without the body's existence.

Once a body has been developed (that is somewhat self-sustaining) upon which the privileged person depends, the general environment outside the body is no longer directly accessible to the privileged person because it only extends over the body, and as a body's complexity grows, the privileged occasions of the central personal society may extend over only some of the body directly. For the "central monad," the body's terminal occasions form a non-personal society whose defining characteristic is a determination created by the central person. This characteristic is found in the initial data of all the next occasions of the body's lower-level persons that are contiguous to the dominant actual occasions of the higher-level personal society. Because of the proximity and self-maintenance of the bodily personal societies, there can also be exchanges of defining characteristics directly amongst the occasions of the body, as well as to and from the dominant person.

The non-personal society at the lowest level of complexity functions as a body, a body that is completely self-sustaining in its dipolar relationship within the cosmic Person, that is, it cannot die: It does not depend for its existence on data from complex occasions that can die. Though it cannot avoid prehending data from the unsurpassable cosmic Person, that Person cannot die either.

The lowest-level society's contribution to a personally ordered society of intermediate complexity is its predictability. The adventure of novel life requires the relative constancy of others. An actual occasion that has risen above the constancy and triviality of the minimally creative contributions presented by its actual world, risks disrupting the organization of the society upon which it depends because those more trivial occasions upon which it depends will in turn be required to prehend the more complex creation.

But an actual entity reaching beyond the minimally enriching satisfactions of the *lowest-level* society cannot disrupt that society so much that it ceases. The creativity of more novel outcomes is always a risk worth taking at this level, a risk that, undoubtedly, has always been taken. Those minimally creative occasions that inherit the more novel outcome will experience the novelty. They will either be threatened by it and devalue its impact on its own satisfaction, or will be enriched by it and feed it back to the society that originated it and any others contiguous to itself. This feedback helps establish a privileged nexus that can both depend on others to provide its basic survival environment and to store the novelty that will eventually establish a higher level of complexity for all involved.

With the establishment of a more complex environment, the personally ordered society is exposed to the possibility of death if something disrupts the bodily environment so much that some member of the central personal nexus cannot integrate the disorder and dies before reaching a determinate, satisfied state.

DEATH OF A PERSON

Whitehead proposes that once an actual entity is established, it must progress to a new determinate being, a superject, for subsequent others. He puts this necessity in Categoreal Obligation i, The Category of Subjective Unity:

> The many feelings which belong to an incomplete phase in the process . . . are compatible for integration by reason of the unity of their subject (*PR* 26). This Category of Subjective Unity is a doctrine of pre-established harmony . . . The many feelings, in any incomplete phase, are necessarily compatible with each other by

reason of their individual conformity to the subjective end evolved for that phase (*PR* 224).

Given the context here, to be "integrated" refers to the final state of the actual entity, namely, its satisfaction, or, as I would rather express it, the actual entity has created a datum for its successor since the successful termination of an actual entity is *not* part of the actual entity itself that created it: It only exists as a changeless part in a contiguous, "privileged" successor, as the privileged datum for that successor. So, if to be "integrated" means to be "satisfied," and if "satisfied" means "to be a part in a successor," what can bring about the death of an intermediate personal society? How can a non-divine personal society have a last member? What does it mean for a personal nexus to "die?"

The concern here is not the death of an actual occasion, what Whitehead after Locke calls its "perishing" or satisfaction. Creativity is the inclusive, life-side of the dipolar moment: the wholeness of a feeling-subject whose goal in life is to enjoy, or feel, what others have determined for it with their perishings and to bring about a fortuitous end to its life as a "dead" being (a momentary life perished) that some others will and must resurrect in their lives. The Ultimate Category states this most fundamental truth: Every *successful* living subject will perish as an object for other subjects: Each of many wholes becomes a part in many wholes, or the most quoted Whiteheadian version, "The many become one, and are increased by one" (*PR* 21). The object that an occasion has created causes new subjects to feel, in part, exactly as the living subject felt at its death.

However, the meaning of "death" in the present context is the "death of a society." There are two kinds of societies, personal and non-personal. In a personal society an actual entity creates a being that is inherited by each successive member of the personal (serial) society. A personal society has memory, a retention that is unique to each member of the society. This memory is not just of a "defining characteristic" that defines all societies, but is the inheritance of the full creation the prior member of the personal series came to be.

In a low-level, non-personal society what others do dominates each member. Each moment inherits the creations of its prior and contiguous neighbors and contributes to all its contiguous successors. Creative enhancement at each moment is at a minimum, so the being that was created at some prior time and is now passed back and forth (as the society survives temporally) continues to dominate the feelings of each new member. No privileged series exists on a more complex level than any of the other occasions in the society. In any case, the lowest-level society in each cosmic epoch exists necessarily and cannot cease.

A non-personal society, however, may also be composed of higher-level personal societies as, for example, the people that make up a nation or a club or the molecules in a rock. These societies are multiplicities of occasions ordered coordinately within any actual occasion that is able to prehend the spatially extended society simultaneously.

To kill a society, whether personal or non-personal, all future members must fail to "materialize," or better, fail to dipolarize. Since non-personal societies are composed of many personal societies, the question comes down to: How is it possible to kill a person? Since the Category of the Ultimate seems best interpreted to say, (1) that many necessarily come to be a new being (by means of the creative and temporally extended process of the actual entity) and, (2) the new being must "become," that is, *be*, the initial, privileged datum of at least one[11] new coming-to-be (by way of the temporally instantaneous "transition"), how can a personal series of actual occasions cease, that is, die?

> An actual entity is to be conceived both as a subject presiding over its own immediacy of becoming, and a superject which is the atomic creature exercising its function of objective immortality. It has become a "being"; and it belongs to the nature of every being that it is a potential for every [sic] "becoming" (*PR* 45). [This hyperbole is qualified later:] It is not true that whatever happens is immediately a condition laid upon everything else (*AI* 198).

If every process of coming to be must succeed in creating a new being, and if every new being must be the primary datum for a new privileged actual entity in a personal society, a personal nexus cannot cease. The options seem forced: Either not every coming-to-be comes to be, or not every being that has come to be is datum for another process, but exits as a self-sustaining being not conditioning a process. The latter is intolerable: The most basic concept of a dipolar, process metaphysic is that coming-to-be is the inclusive term; being cannot exist alone. Being is always a part of,

---

11. Normally the satisfaction/superject initiates only one successor, say N, that is, it is the privileged datum for only one immediate successor since other beings created by others have either already become parts in other new wholes or will come to be after N begins. However, there may be exceptions when it comes to explaining "entanglement."

that is, conditioning, some dipolar, processing whole or other as all of the epochal Categories declare.

The solution must be that the final actual entity in a personal nexus that dies is one that does not reach a satisfied determination. If every satisfied subject must be a superject in a new dipolar moment of a personal series, no personal series can end with a satisfaction because the state of satisfaction is necessarily an objective datum for a new occasion, as the Category of the Ultimate expresses. The only other option for ending a personal nexus is to allow the last occasion to begin but to give up before reaching a satisfaction. Why would it give up?

This new occasion must not only include the satisfaction of the immediately prior member of its series, that is, its privileged datum, but it must also include any and all immediately prior and contiguous actual entities' superjects. If all these inheritances are not fortuitously ordered, they will present their mutual disarray within the new nascent subject. A generic, subjective aim is established that must include all the disorderly initial data. The subject struggles to fulfill the aim, that is, to make a new specified determination that must somehow include all it began with, but the suffering and effort required may be more than the moment can handle, so the occasion gives up, and with its failure the personal series comes to an end. This is not to deny the possibility of a temporary death, whereby the personal series can begin again if the body is not too degraded.

The prior successful actualizations of the person are not gone even if the personal series cannot retain them itself, since they are vaguely retained by subordinate, contiguous fragmentary occasions, and always retained as they are by the cosmically inclusive Person who would have necessarily prehended the last datum the person created—the datum that initiated and was sustained for a moment by the unsuccessful occasion that ended/killed the personal society.

The death of a non-personal, intermediate level society composed of fragmentary persons requires the death of all the individuals. Since a fragmentary personal nexus need not have any set number of actual entities in its lifetime, and since empirical evidence suggest that physical entities apart from "empty" space are more or less personally ordered series, for these societies to cease, the strands of personal order must cease. But whether or not they do and how cannot be settled on Categoreal grounds.

What can be determined by an appeal to metaphysical principles is the primordiality and everlastingness of the lowest-level, fragmentary, non-personal nexus. Since all members of reality are necessarily dipolar, "whether that instance be God or an actual occasion of the world" (*PR* 36), there must be fragmentary occasions, those "of the world," to create objects for the all-inclusive Subject. Since every member of the lowest-level society is somewhat as it is because of its self-creativity, no matter how minimal that is, no fragmentary occasion must exist just as it does. Every fragmentary occasion exists as it does because of contingent conditions. Actually, no *particular* fragmentary occasion must even exist at all. Nevertheless, some fragmentary occasions *or other* are necessary (Category M4). The class of lowest-level occasions cannot be empty; there must always be some in process: there must always be new fragmentary objects created.

In a similar way, no particular divine, non-fragmentary Actual Entity must exist since all actual entities are contingent; still it is necessary that there always be some supreme Actual Entity or other in process in the cosmic personal Society (Category M3). The class of cosmically all-inclusive actual entities cannot be empty; there must always be one in process. More than one supreme at each moment is logically impossible. Each supreme One must include all actualized others, including the superject of the previous all-inclusive process. Since there can only be one Actual Entity that is all-inclusive at each moment, each all-inclusive moment must be a member of a personal Society.

So though death is inevitable for most societies, two societies cannot die: the lowest-level which supports all other higher-level societies, and the highest-level personal Society that integrates and preserves all accomplishments, the personal society that gives meaning to "*uni*-verse." Neither could either of these two societies been created: They could never come into existence, since they exist necessarily. Though these two societies are primordial and everlasting, every actual entity maintaining these societies is created. The members of these two societies do exhibit Whitehead's first Categoreal Obligation, Subjective Unity, each in its own way: For divinity, each moment must begin with the satisfaction/datum of its predecessor, and end as a satisfied/datum for its successor; for the lowest-level society, some moments *or other* must begin, and some or other must end satisfied. The lowest-level, non-personal society as a whole cannot die since it would destroy the dipolarity of the Unsurpassable. All intermediate societies can and will eventually die, or evolve into new societies.

There can be one and only be one unsurpassed actual entity each moment in the Unsurpassable's personal nexus, but is there a set number, a finite number, of lowest-level occasions "in unison of becoming" at each moment? Even though each actual occasion of the lowest-level personal strands may begin before or after any other, each minimal strand is always in process (as is every personal nexus) since the transition from one process to the next is extensionless. Each actual entity is born and perishes, but creative process is continuous from one moment to the next. So to put the question another way, are there a set number of personal strands at the lowest level?

The only way the number could be reduced is for some occasion to fail to create a determinate satisfaction (that is, to create a (privileged) datum for its immediate successor), or under special, seemingly unstable conditions, several may terminate simultaneously as initial data for one process, but I'm inclined to think this may happen only at the intermediate level of creative complexity since this is more likely the existential property of intermediate-level occasions. If lowest-level occasions could die unsatisfied, what metaphysical criterion would set the limit on how many could die and still have sufficient numbers to satisfy the dipolarity required by the Modal Categories?

On the other hand, can there be in increase in the number of contemporaneous, minimal-level personal strands? Perhaps a personal nexus may be able to terminate in two successors as a way of avoiding failure to reach a satisfaction due to internal conflict, which would increase the number of contemporaneous occasions. An increase in number implies a finite number to begin with. If there has never been a first member in the Unsurpassable nexus, and, therefore, also no first members in the lowest-level society, temporally the actual entities must be innumerable. But spatially, that is, coordinately, an infinity of occasions (innumerable actualities) would seem to be the denial that one Actual Entity at each moment could extend over all and be the Subject of all contemporaneously created objects.

CONTINGENT COMPLEXITY

The gain in complexity and possible enrichment of intermediate-level societies comes at a cost: The body can become too disordered to sustain the dominant person, and the higher level of possible experiential richness can also bring a higher level of suffering.

How and why do occasions group together in ways that the lowest-level society doesn't but undergirds? First of all, a universe with only the

Unsurpassable and the minimally complex society as its dipolar subordinate is a mythical structure. These two societies must exist whereas all others may not, but given the freedom of occasions to experiment somewhat with their data, and given that there is always divine influence flowing into the datum of every actual occasion, and finally given the objective or metaphysical aim that enrichment is the goal, it seems unlikely that there ever was a time when only the metaphysically existing societies existed.

"In the beginning" of the rise of contingent complexity, an actual occasion, say B in a personal series x, would have begun as always with the termination of another, A. Since there is no contingent complexity to disrupt at this lowest level and bring about its death by failure, every actual entity that begins would end with a new determination (Whitehead's theory of Categoreal Obligation i) and every determination can only exist by initiating a new actual entity (Category of the Ultimate). Other occasions (in other personal societies) would have begun just before B began. Their initial data consist of beings not created by A. Even though K in society y, M in z, and so on, are already in process as B begins, their initial data, if contiguous to B, must also be part of B's initial datum since all beings are public. Though beings K, M, etc., are a parts of other processes, they are still available to flow into any nascent actual entity contiguous to them. B simultaneously prehends a multiplicity of determinations, which is what always happens even at the lowest possible level. The contiguousness of the last divine creation is also always part of the multiplicity of beings that are B's datum.

However, to rise to another level of complexity, the next occasion after B, namely, C, in the personal nexus, x, must prehend B's superject that includes A and all other Ls and Ns that were contiguous to B at the lowest societal level. C in the x-nexus simultaneously extends over more actualizations than other occasions in the lowest-level, non-personal society composed of minimally creative personal strands.

Picture, for an analogy, a two-dimensional hexagon as the coordinate shape of six superjects to be inherited by B since with B in the center (creating with what it inherited from A), the six occasions can be horizontally contiguous to B. The next temporal moment, moving vertically, is C, the privileged occasion that inherits B's superject/creation. Six other occasions of the hexagon can be contiguous to B's satisfaction and include it, even though they begin at slightly different times, so long as C is maintaining B's created being for the other six which it is doing as the privileged occasion in

Birth and Death of Hierarchal Relationships

the group. So at the lowest-level society six occasions will be contiguous to B's superject. But if one considers that the personal nexus, x, of A through C is occurring vertically to B's hexagonal satisfaction, C will be contiguous to B's creation. B's successor, C, will be contiguous not just to what B created, but to all the six other creations that had begun just before B began if they also "moved" temporally along with C. Perhaps for no particular reason (which is why this is a contingent or accidental occurrence) some of the personal strands that provided data for occasions in the x-nexus remain spatially motionless relative to x.

The x-nexus is more complex than its neighbors, so when the members of the x-nexus are prehended by members in its neighboring personal societies, they will be more complex than those occasions in the larger environment not prehending members of the x-nexus. If the complexity is enriching, it will be attractive, tending to help maintain a symbiotic relationship wherein the societies providing data for the more dominant personal society are insulating that society from the wider lowest-level environment and receiving input from their more complex higher-level neighbor. Both the non-personal society, now becoming a body, and the personal society that influences others to continue to contribute to its personal series, are rewarded by the fortunate relationships. Both are more enriched than the environment from which they arose; though the x-nexus is rewarded with the more enriched experience. This society, however, faces an eventual death since no contingent grouping will continue forever.

For the first time, in this account, there is meaning to being "at rest" and, therefore, also being "in motion" relative to that x-nexus which is considered at rest. Of course, "at rest" can also mean "unaccelerated motion." Inertia has entered into the world. The bodily occasions no longer randomly occur as easily here or there as the occasions do in the lowest-level society. There is a perpetuation of an enriched past for the dominant society and a reason to keep the bodily societies at rest relative to itself in order to insure its own survival and enrichment. But when the embodied personal society does move to another region of the environment, how does it accomplish this?

Chapter 11

Movement within Non-Moving Wholes

MOVEMENT

ATOMISM OF THE DEMOCRITIAN type has been so popular because of its common sense explanation of "change." Particles remain the same as they rearrange their distances from each other. Change is seen simply as the rearrangement of units that retain their self-identity through the rearrangement. Amongst the problems, however, that such a theory faces, apart from its usual championing of determinism, is the inability to make sense of "*rearrangement*" because there is no place where any "arrangement" can exist. An "arrangement" is a contrast amongst many items. This contrast requires a whole to exist that can simultaneously extend over and compare the many contrasting parts. Consciousness of the comparison is not required, but a whole with parts simultaneously compared is.

"Space," in the atomists' theory, seems to be the only possible whole that can simultaneously embrace many, but "space" is either "nothing" or can mysteriously remain the same whole with successively different parts as new arrangements occur within it. Further, since the old arrangement no longer exists when the atoms rearrange, nothing exists to compare the "new" arrangement to. No arrangement can be called "new" unless there is something old, that is, prior, to compare it to. Even if somehow two arrangements could be compared, there is nothing in such an atomistic metaphysic to meaningfully define "temporal sequence." Differences alone do not imply sequential differences of the "same thing" that is sequentially changing.

An event metaphysic must deny that substance moves or changes. Each "substance," that is, each dipolar unit of creative process, creates during a finite temporal extension, as it extends over the accomplishments of many others simultaneously. Its spatial extensiveness or volume is where it is, and its temporal duration is the effort it takes to do what it does. As it progresses towards an accomplishment, it can compare what it might become to what it inherited. Given a longer inherited history, it can compare recent past to less recent past accomplishments and know which came earlier because what happened first is a part mediated by what contains it. An actual occasion can allow an historical vector to continue with little alteration, or it can make an effort to alter it. Herein lies the difference between experiences described by Special Relativity, concerned with constant perpetuation, and General Relativity concerned with an altered direction.

One can't be sure that the spatial-temporal dilations physicists conjecture and observe are metaphysical or merely contingencies exhibited by our cosmic epoch, but there seems something very fundamental about the need for one whole to simultaneously contain many, and for each moment to require enough temporal extension to allow an effort to bring about a new accomplishment, if it is successful. Actual entities exhibit spatiality (whatever the number of dimensions involved in its geometry) and temporality. Every actual entity takes its own "time" to occur, and every personal series of actual entities is either at rest or moving (changing position) relative to its own past.

Special Relativity describes the affect different perspectives dictate for a personal series relative to others at rest with it or moving unaccelerated relative to it. Just as objects have different phenomenal shapes from different points of view in three dimensions, so too do objects appear to have different sizes and temporal extensions in four dimensions. The apparent changes in four-dimensional objects are the result of the finite transmission rate of information from one personal society to another personal society moving unaccelerated relative to each other. The Lorentz transformation formulas allow one to translate from one perspective to another, just as one can interpret the oval shape of a coin experienced from one perspective in three dimensions to be circular from another perspective.

With unaccelerated or constant motion, there are no ontological changes in the actual entities carrying the objects defining the personal societies moving relative to each other. When an object survives from moment to moment, the actual occasions of the personal society that include it set up anticipations of where it will be in following moments, that is, they contain projection vectors which cause expectations that the past datum will continue as is into the future. An effort over and above the minimal effort required to maintain the object's inertia, is required to prevent the projections from being fulfilled. This effort is an "acceleration;" it changes what would have occurred if no additional effort is made to change the anticipated satisfaction. The occasions exerting the additional effort take more time to complete their effort than they would just to maintain the inertial expectations.

Two parallel projectors will remain parallel and the same distance apart from one moment to the next when the personal nexus remains at rest; however, any effort to change the location of the at-rest projections must bend the projections (cause them to lean to one side relative to the fixed past) creating a parallelogram. The projectors will be closer together than they were before the acceleration. The occasion is spatially shortened in the direction the effort was applied. The theoretical limit would be a projection at right angles to the past, which would indicate the impossible, infinite acceleration.

In many past theories, "motion" or change of spatial position of a substance, has been a metaphysical given. The analogy in a process, event philosophy is to see "motion," as adding something new to the past. In this sense everything that survives "moves" from the past to the present. Motion only makes sense as contrasted to rest. The multiplicity of actual entities that comprise the universe are not at rest relative to the debunked "ether" or "absolute space" or the edge of the cosmos or the most distant stars, or even the Big Bang as commonly understood. Rather, each dipolar actual occasion carries some of the unalterable past as its subordinate pole; it is or isn't at rest relative to its own past. If there were no changes in the actual occasions' coordinate contrasts, every occasion in the present would be at spatial rest relative to its past, even though it might "move" along other qualitative dimensions.

Radiation is merely a series of personal societies carrying an object, each from its own perspective that remains at rest in in its own personal society. If the "object" is "massless," it is carried forward in each personal society at the fastest possible rate so no interaction is possible between occasions amongst the members of the society whose data include the original object being radiated. The radiation is performed by the lowest-level society in which the object can exist. The low-level personal societies that initially inherited the object, spread the object in all directions in which contiguous occasions exist, not by moving the being, but by perspectival inheritance of the object. No object/superject moves, but its influence exists wherever actual entities overlap its region, either directly or by way of intermediaries.

"Movement" more commonly refers to objects not at rest relative to a stationary, that is, unaccelerated, personal series. The movement is traceable through a series of datum inputs to the personal series. For this to be possible the changing positions of the prehended motion must be less than the fastest possible. There are two ways a moving object can provide successive data for a personal nexus: Either (1) by having the object "carried to," that is, mediated by, other actual occasions between the "moving" object and the personal series prehending the object, or (2) by having the at-rest personal nexus extend over the object in the moving society so it is directly prehended at successive different places at successive times. This is what always happens within the cosmically inclusive personal nexus since each cosmic actual entity extends over all objects each moment.

The defining object of an intermediately complex personal society resists being merely radiated away because the personal society has developed a body more complex than that which lowest-level occasions have. This body sits between the privileged occasions of the personal series and the lower level occasions that carry the radiated objects. There is feedback between the body organized to support the higher-level personal society and the personal society itself. The level of complexity of body parts can only be maintained if they can charm their subordinate societies to maintain a certain level of stability.

A MOVING SOCIETY

To move a person who lives dependent on a body, requires moving the body. The body can only move if the occasions in the societies composing the body are able to interact with the environment with sufficient intensity to alter future members of their societies. In the extensive region occupied by the body and its privileged personal society, the lowest-level society still exists. Higher-level societies do not replace lower level societies; they continue to depend on them as they build their more complex contrasts. If a high-level society ceases, that does not mean the lower-level societies must also cease, though many will without the influence of the higher-level organization, exempting, as always, the necessary existence of the lowest-level society. Occasions at every level are contiguous to all higher-level societies that extent over and include them, though the major influence higher-level societies have on lower ones seems to be mediated by intermediate societies.

The kind of influence that is effective within some intermediate societies is known in physics as a "force:" Strong, weak, electromagnetic and gravitational forces are well-known. In our cosmic epoch these are the forces exhibited by the societies most evident in the composition of macroscopic bodies. Undoubtedly there are other forces if it be true that all that occurs within a cell or a brain cannot be reduced to the atomic and molecular forces. This is not to say that there are cellular activities that are apart from atoms, but the behavior of atoms is someone modified within the wholeness of the cell due to atomic societies also prehending the contiguous being each occasion of a cellular society creates.

Yet, it is an empirical issue to determine where wholes and their superjects exist (and whether or not they are organized personally). However, there can be no doubt that human experience, visual experience, for example, is not merely cellular or atomic in nature. Simultaneously, many colored shapes are experienced involving a spatial extent and a qualitative diversity not attributable to any one atom or cell. A multiplicity of atomic entities is at most a non-personal society wherein each member has no over-arching, simultaneous experience of the many. Whether the units are subatomic, atomic, molecular or cellular, a metaphysic that doesn't require the "atoms" of multiplicities to be simultaneously embraced by more inclusive wholes can never make sense of comparison and change.

Nor can one doubt that atoms and molecules behave differently in my hands, as I type, from how they would if I were playing ball. If I'm not pathological, my human personal society does cause my fingers to do things but only because I can persuade my brain's cellular societies and they in turn to persuade the atomic societies, and they the subatomic societies, to somewhat modify their own inertia. Most of what I call my "body" is not contiguous to my personal nexus. Even that part of my brain that is directly affected by me is not all that much affected by me. The brain for the most part goes on doing its own thing.

The animal body is an organization of many societies. The brain, or some aspect of the brain, forms a non-personal society that is a complex datum at each moment for me. As soon as I have brought a new determination

Movement within Non-Moving Wholes

into being, that non-personal society in my brain has new data for its own processes. What I create is undoubtedly contiguous to many other cells and subcellular events, but they are not as responsive as the cells developed to interact with me. The datum I create becomes data for many brain cells and alters each cell which in turn alters somewhat the electro-chemical composition of the cell's body which in turn alters chemicals that alter other cells (particularly neighboring nerve cells). Eventually the chain of nerve cell alterations causes changes in muscles. The chain of events causes movement of part of my extended body. The other parts of my extended body which are prehending each other (so they are electro-chemically and atomically bonded with each other), causes the other parts of my body to move when one part does.

MASS AND ACCELERATION

Since human experience requires a body, and since much (all?) of what humans experience is other bodies, speculation on the nature of reality has been biased towards considering bodies as the fundamental stuff of reality with all the attributes materialistic metaphysics have articulated. Motion is thus seen as transposition of a self-identical thing from one place in "space" to another. But in process metaphysics, bodies are created. They are not only contingent in how they exist, but in whether or not they exist.

The underlying metaphysical state, that is, the only condition that seems unavoidably necessary, is the existence of a base society of actual occasions which in our cosmic epoch seems to be "space." The only "bodies" in this spatial society are those beings created by prior and contiguous neighbors. Each actual occasion's creation is "handed" to contiguous successors. Every creation is scattered effortlessly as fast as possible to other nascent occasions. No bodies exist except the momentary bodies of contiguous neighbors' superjects. "Mass" does not exist, only radiation, the uninhibited transfer of the pasts' satisfactions to those in the future.

Mass only exists when effort is exerted to prevent uninhibited radiation. An enduring body only exists within an "enduring mind" which in event metaphysics means some higher-level personal order must exist to maintain the body. This personal social order must also be more complex than the minimal personal strands required by the Category of the Ultimate. There must be an intermediate-level occasion that begins its existence with the satisfaction of prior actual entities in the lowest-level nexus (as do all occasions at that level), but this particular strand of personal order creates an outcome for its successors more complex than its other contiguous neighbors, one of which inherits the satisfaction without perspective. This successor's datum is somewhat privileged: It is still simultaneously conditioned by more than one other contiguous subordinate, and, in turn, simultaneously conditions the many contiguous members of its subordinate societies, but only one of the successors must begin with the more complex creation. The contiguous beings created by other successors could be created somewhat earlier, and kept in existence by other personal strands.

At first this successive give and take of influence is minimal and sporadic, but they mutually reinforce each other until the bodily occasions "desire" to be influenced by each momentary whole they help condition, and the mentality of the enduring subject becomes more adept at how to partially control them. The very existence of each momentary subject depends on the successful perpetuation of the body's structure. Nothing can guarantee the body will perpetually support the subjects of the dominant personal society. In fact, every such structure will eventually fail; and the more complex the mutual arrangement, the more likely it is to fail since it depends on more and more specialized societies that cannot readily survive environmental alterations.

Once cooperation amongst the body's occasions and between the body and the dominant personal order is sufficient to maintain a life history, "at rest" becomes meaningful as the minimum effort required to create a new dominant subject in the personal nexus. The data from the body's occasions persists in the "same place" in successive dominant subjects. The past's coordinate structure is projected into the future as part of the subject's conditional, subjective aim. The personal nexus is at rest when that projection is fulfilled.

A personal nexus could also be said to be moving uniformly as seen from the perspective of another personal series. Special Relativity makes clear that unaccelerated linear motion or being at rest is merely a difference of perspective. At rest only requires a minimum effort to maintain the status quo: Inertia rules. But inertia only exists if something exists with mass to resist change. Mass is the resistance. It is the effort required to maintain the status quo. It is the effort required to keep subordinates from straying too far.

Control of others is always partial. An electron in "empty" space will behave differently from one more or less bound to a proton in a hydrogen atom. Yet the bound electron still has some freedom to maintain its self-identity, pulsating behavior and even location, but the atom must constantly "accelerate" the electron around the proton, that is, the electron is continually changing its projected "at rest" course either because at each moment its newly inherited data (provided by the atom) alters its subjective aim. Or, perhaps, it is partly because what the electron "desires" is to remain bound to the proton because its subjective feelings are richer when it is.

Any movement that is not linear, that is, not at rest, is movement that changes the inertial course of a personal society: Motion describes a directional deviation from the past's perpetuation. The sharper the deviation is from the inertia of the past, the more energy required to execute the change. When the change of direction is repeated and forms a consistent pattern, such as the course a bound electron takes around the proton in a hydrogen atom, constant acceleration is possible without disrupting a larger pattern, like a water molecule, that depends on the bound hydrogen society. The longevity of a proton in its turn depends on the patterned energy of its bound quarks, as they themselves may depend on subordinate others, right down to the lowest society of "empty" spatial occasions.

Acceleration is the key to creating mass: Constant acceleration is the key to maintaining mass. Without acceleration all created satisfaction/superjects would pass effortlessly from one moment to the next as fast as they occur and pass the created characteristic as far as each occasion spatially extends. This is why massless events radiate at the fastest transmission speed possible. Effort expended to slow down the transmission reveals itself as mass. Mass provides reality with persistence that can provide richness and strength.

General Relativity theory is based on the equivalence of acceleration and gravity. Gravity affects actual occasions in the same way as acceleration. The process of an actual occasion that is changing direction takes longer to occur than it would have taken to remain at rest. Relative to the occasions of the past members of the personal society that remain at rest, the accelerating occasion must work harder to bring about the new position. An occasion in a gravitational field must work against the affect of mass. The affect of mass is to create an environment that is denser than a relatively gravity-free region. The data for occasions in a gravitational region will be more complex requiring greater effort, a longer time, to create a new outcome.

Einstein's insight on General Relativity is tied to his concept of the spatial-temporal continuum. So long as the unity of the universe is thought to be space, space itself must vary its "density" or, in his language, "curvature." The one space of the universe as it is at one moment, is somehow the same one space but different in following moments after motion has occurred. Einstein could not conceive of Reality being a new one, a new whole, each moment. Mass does change "space," not by altering the one "space," but by radiating into the environment conditions that do not exist in a relatively massless environment. All indications are that what mass radiates, that is, what a region of mass gives as data for actual occasions around the massive society, is seductive: Its data is attractive: It causes actual occasions to accelerate towards the massive society.

MEASUREMENT

Since acceleration is movement that does not continue the inertial straight lines from the past, "straightness" requires a definition. Whitehead noted that the operational definition (that a straight line is the path of an unaccelerated light particle), is circular. A definition must be independent of physical processes in order to determine whether or not a physical path is straight or curved, that is, at rest or accelerated. Whitehead's definition of "straightness" begins with a definition of an ovate class. Any member of the class can only intersect another member once. As an example, think of two circles partially overlapping with a common intersect as in a Venn diagram. Only one such intersect is possible. The intersect itself is another oval with two unique points, A and B, where the circumference of the two circles cross. A straight line between A and B is the tail end of an "abstractive set" formed by ovals nested within the intersect, all of which have points A and B in common.

This definitional procedure can be applied to any number of dimensions. In fact a "point" is the limit of an abstractive set of ovals nested one within the other all of which have only one region in common. Since "nothing" can actually exist, that is, no actual occasion can be a non-extended region, a "point" is a region as small as one cares to push the abstractive set which in principle can always be smaller, but never zero. One does not develop volume by amassing non-extended points. "Points" are arbitrarily small regions of finitely extended volumes.

Movement within Non-Moving Wholes

Having a definition of "straightness" or "flatness" in some dimension is not enough information to carry out measurements, the essential activity of empirical investigation. Measurement depends on a finite unit being the same unit in *different* times and places. The inches along a ruler are not coincident since they are in different places. One might try to confirm that the inches are the same length by cutting the ruler up and placing all the inches coincident, but then only an inch can be measured. Replacing the inches end to end raises the original concern: Are they all the same length now that they have been moved? In fact, if Einstein is right and space has a different metric in different places, the non-coincident inches are not the same length.

The problem can be heightened by noticing that when one places a ruler along side an object to be measured, one must be certain that both ends of the object are coincident with two points on the ruler, say zero and ten inches. One must observe one end, and then the other, but what if the ruler moved from the first end when looking at the second end? That this is so often the case has given rise to such platitudes as "Measure twice; cut once." Yet, the theoretical issue is not settled by resting comfortable with a faith that measuring devices are not elastic or much affected by their environment, at least in ways not controllable like pressure and temperature. As much as one tests the measuring devices with other devices, sooner or later all meaningful measurements are based on the one thing that cannot change, the past, and on the one thing that can simultaneously compare the past to the present or one aspect of the past to another, direct introspection, introspection by a subject (1) capable of simultaneously experiencing both the past and present and (2) capable of simultaneously extending over a present extensive enough to contain the object being measured.

Empirical science is completely based on the retention of the changeless past into the present and the ability to simultaneously compare two aspects of one extended, present whole. Every change is a difference between one state of a nexus and a successive state of the same nexus. Science, that is, depends on the ability to simultaneously compare successive differences of the "same thing," a "thing" which exhibits both temporal and spatial extensiveness. Introspection with some awareness can only take place, so far as we know, in actual occasions that have greatly simplified their initial datum, simplified it enough to give rise to Presentational Immediacy. This simplification is the bane of empirical knowledge. Not giving this simplifying process its due gives rise to the Fallacy of Misplaced Concreteness.

Einstein fell into this error in his formulation of the General Theory of Relativity and his denial that fully concrete actual occasions could have any degree of freedom of self-determination.

Every change is acceleration along some dimension resulting in a difference from the past. Spatial change requires the present to do something other than repeat the spatial arrangement of the past. Each actual entity in a personal series repeats some or all of the past of the personal nexus as well as including in its data other neighboring beings contiguous to its initiation. In total, every actual entity's initial data is a multiplicity, a non-personal nexus. If the personal society is moving *without acceleration*, it will repeat or continue to fulfill its past's spatial projections, but will have new neighbors added in at the initiation of each new actual occasion in the personal series.

ENERGY

"Energy," like "extension" and "quality," is so fundamental that attempts to define it can do little more than use synonyms or point at examples. This so because "energy" is ultimately one side of the Category of the Ultimate: "Energy" is "coming-to-be." But even though coming-to-be is not being, energy is never just energy; it is always found as this kind of energy as opposed that kind. It is either photonic, electronic or anti-protonic, human or divine. No matter how miniscule or cosmic in scope, energy begins with something that is this, not that, and "transforms" it *by additions* into a somewhat new being. "Energy" is effort bringing into being a quantity of some quality, somewhat like and somewhat different from what already exists.

A "being," on the other hand, can likewise never be found alone: Every being is what it is because it is qualifying comings-to-be. Every being is a simultaneous contrast of qualities. It is a quantity, a quantum of coordinated extension. It is not merely a quantity of extension, a quantity of a quantity. It is a quantity of a quality; or more accurately, a quantity of many contrasting qualities. These externally related quantities define the spatiality of the actual entity in abstraction from the whole spatial-temporal moment. So in the attempt to understand the relationship of energy and mass so elegantly expressed in Einstein's formula, $E=mc^2$, one must be careful not to equate the energy of an actual entity with the actual entity. Reality is always dipolar.

So neither can the energy of the actual entity be understood as the being or beings supported by, or contained in, the actual entity. Temporality and spatiality are two irreducible dimensions, exhibited by all actual entities, that can never be collapsed one into the other. Sequence is not coordination: Process is nothing without something to process; and what is processed must be the result of a process: It can never just be. Spatial extension without temporal extension is as meaningless as time without space: A subject without objects is as meaningless as an object not functioning as an object for a subject. (Categories E1, E2, and E3, Principles of Dipolar Epochal Universality).

In the lowest-level society of actual occasions, occasions exist inheriting and slightly modifying the quantified qualities they feel. The initial data of each arrives from those just prior and contiguous to its birth. One prior actual occasion's termination is only possible because another begins with the prior's determination. This is not to deny that other beings, supported by other actual occasions in its neighborhood are also included in its initial data. These lowest-level occasions inherit and pass on to their successors their quality of feeling with no inhibitions. The energy of the moment, in this "empty space," is at the lowest possible level. Little is changing; maintenance is king: What is inherited is passed on, and what is passed on radiates to others as fast as possible, that is, as fast as the temporal epoch of the occasions in the society occur which is always some finite rate.

In this mythically ideal state, qualities "move" as fast as possible, but none are accelerated by the occasions they are qualifying nor affected by gravity. However, the insights of quantum mechanics assure us that this low-level society can never be completely homogeneous. Occasions spontaneously generate conditions that stand out as more complex. In the language of physics, there are quantum fluctuations in the perfect vacuum that spontaneously bring about ("create") virtual particles. These "particles" occur apparently in pairs such that one member of the pair can stand out against the "vacuum" because its uniqueness is maintained for a moment at the expense of another whose uniqueness falls below the vacuum's average. The moment these societal aberrations survive is no longer than the epochal durations of the members of the society. They are usually doomed to unite in a common datum for the next occasion: They "annihilate" each other.

So this mythical society consists of qualities being inherited by each occasion from many others. If the society is rather isolated from other societies, the quality passed around will be very much the same, but never exactly the same because they are always massaged by the process energy each has which is always somewhat indeterminate as to its outcome. But considering the characteristics of a nearly perfect vacuum society may help one see that "nothingness" is meaningless and that cosmic wholeness cannot fail to have something to unify, even though the extreme symmetry such a society would have could never be actualized. Reality is asymmetrical; a completely homogeneous vacuum is not possible. This is true because every occasion must be somewhat unique. The experience of homogeneity is always the result of failing to experience the uniqueness of each moment or ignoring it, committing the Fallacy of Misplaced Concreteness. When occasionally the uniquenesses of many occasions are found as data for another, the possibility exists for an outcome that does not get swallowed up by the monotony of the herd.

This seems to happen when the virtual particles are infused with energy, that is, when vectored beings form a field that accelerates an occasion by changing its inertial outcome. Pulsation seems to be a necessary characteristic of any low-level enduring society. Changing the intensity of a being allows the satisfaction of an occasion to be somewhat different from the feeling initiating the occasion, without creating a new quality. But spatial reorientation can occur even before it is clear that "at rest" or "in constant motion" makes sense. "At rest" and "in constant motion" are concepts that likely make sense only in relation to other occasions, probably personal societies of occasions with some consistent perpetuation.

But "spin" requires the occasion to change its orientation relative to its own past. Thus spin appears as a characteristic of personal societies that persist for some time even before orbital motion. Apart from details that depend on the present state of particle physics, the general principle that comes into play here is that acceleration in a constant cyclical fashion requires effort, but an effort that is localized. Rather than allowing the vacuum occasions to radiate their superject/beings effortlessly throughout the society, an occasion, or series of occasions are continually reining in the "at rest" radiation by bending its low-energy path into a higher-energy path. The energy comes not from the processes of others, but from the enriched and enriching data they place at the inception of the process that will alter its outcome due to the influence of the beings from its past. The occasion must work harder to bring about a satisfactory result because it is saddled with more and weightier data. It may not succeed, though low-level societies seldom generate sufficient novelty to overwhelm an occasion so much like themselves.

"Mass" is captured energy, or perhaps it would be better to say mass is captured being whose projected "at rest" position is constantly altered, that is, accelerated to a different relationship (in its contribution to the next satisfaction) with its own past. Every form of constant acceleration is a form of restriction on the occasion's free development which requires more effort to sustain. When the vacuum occasions create virtual particles that become real particles spinning, a consistent personal series is maintained and more mass exists. But even so, the occasions maintaining the more massive particles cannot stop all others from inheriting from the satisfactions created by the enduring particle. Electronic societies pass on electronic beings in a more or less personal relationship, but the field surrounding the electron inherits magnetic qualities. These qualities can in turn accelerate electrons in directions other than the atomic orbits they usually inhabit.

Chapter 12

Entanglement's Challenge to Metaphysics

LOCALITY

Much has been made here of the necessity for actual entities to be contiguous to beings, namely, superjects created by prior actual entities, in order to prehend those creations; and if an actual entity is contiguous to previously created beings, it must prehend them. So how can the process metaphysic presented here interpret what Einstein called "spooky action at a distance," supposedly non-contiguous causation? The issue arises because quantum mechanics allows "particles" to be entangled and then separated sufficiently distant that nothing can be transmitted between them even at the speed of light. Yet, when one of the particles is disturbed so that the entanglement ceases, the other particle is immediately affected. Physicists call such behavior "non-local" influence, causation that seems to occur without the cause being contiguous to the effect. The reality of this non-local influence seems to fly in the face of common sense; but does it? Non-locality, at least for shorter distances, is exactly what common sense assumes and what Einstein's relativity theory discounts, at least for larger distances.

For an example, when one holds a rod on one end and pokes it at something, one's common sense assumes (if one were to think about it) that the far end of the rod moves *at the same time* as the end being held. Transmission of the poke from the held end to the far end does not seem to require a temporal lapse. Likewise, in the old atomistic theories, when a large, round Democritean atom is struck by another, the whole atom moves immediately and simultaneously. Every part of the struck atom moves *at the same time*. The atom is assumed to be a whole, and common sense accepts that every part of a whole moves simultaneously together. Anything that affects the whole affects the complete whole, not just the part of the whole acted upon. Einstein's relativity theory, on the other hand, holds that the rod does not move at the far end until the force has been transmitted at a finite rate to the far end. Likewise, the parts of an "atom" not struck must wait until the force is transmitted through the atom before they can move.

Here we face a *reductio ad absurdum*. The middle of the rod can't move until the rod's first quarter moves, and so on. The only way to avoid Zeno's paradox is to have a smallest unit of movement of finite size; and Albert Einstein (with Max Planck) discovered just such a unit: Transmission is not continuous: It comes in quanta, all or none units. These units are the wholes; one has a complete whole or nothing at all. This is the metaphysical truth embodied in the theory of actual entities.

Common sense is right (though it often commits the Fallacy of Misplaced Concreteness by assuming a large aggregate is a whole): A whole is the simultaneous prehender of the members of an aggregate. Each member of the aggregate could also be the result of a whole. Mistaking an aggregate of many creations for one whole's creation is only possible for higher-level actual occasions (or personal societies of occasions) wherein the datum of Causal Efficacy has been simplified, allowing for the clarity of Presentational Immediacy's strain locus to be projected by Symbolic Reference onto the complex world of one's contemporaries.

So, "locality" has to do with wholes, what is in one whole or the result of one whole. "Non-locality" has to do with one whole's created being (its satisfied determination) supposedly having a causal effect in another whole that is not contiguous to it. "Non-locality" does not mean that what affects one part of a whole affects other aspects of the whole simultaneously; that is what "local" means.

PRIVILEGED ACTUAL ENTITIES AND ENTANGLEMENT

A "privileged" actual entity is one that begins with the satisfaction of an immediately prior actual entity. The prior actual entity can only end if another begins with its creation since the creation, a being, cannot exist on its own. A being is a conditioning of process or it is nothing. Of course, process without it being conditioned by beings is also nothing. This is the necessary dipolarity of reality. Other beings, besides the one that ends a prior process, must also be included, but these others first exist as conditionings of other processes that began earlier but are contiguous to the privileged actual entity.

In the present conjecture about the nature of entanglement, no claim is made that it is anything other than a contingent possibility that occasions can employ to relate to each other. However, that reality has privileged actual entities is a metaphysical necessity: Every successful actual entity of whatever complexity and modality must reach its satisfaction as a datum for another actual entity. What would happen, however, if it were possible for two (or more) actual entities to terminate in the same succeeding actual entity? A privileged actual entity takes no perspective on its satisfied predecessor, since it begins by feeling just what its predecessor became (along with any contiguous others), therefore, its datum (as the subjective aim) emphasizes the feelings that its satisfied predecessor created or passed on to the next member of the personal society formed by the series of privileged actual entities. But if two (or more) predecessors were to reach their satisfactions as data for one privileged actual entity, there would be the tendency to have two aims. Of course, two aims means there are two actual entities, so if the successor is to remain one whole, the two tendencies must be subordinated to the needs of one aim.

Attempts to probe the personal series of wholes that pass on the tendency to be two personal societies ("particles") can disrupt the possibility for the personal series to pass on the delicate balance within the series of wholes. Each whole of the personal society has an internal give and take between the two dominant aspects of its process that new environmental data can destroy. When that happens, the personal nexus of wholes with multiple tendencies, subordinated to one aim, dies, unable to fulfill its single aim; but it perishes giving birth to two privileged actual entities each with its own aim that initiates two personal societies at whatever spatial location they find themselves.

ENTANGLEMENT

The wholes physicists are familiar with seem to be very small, but they are not non-extended "points." Just a moment's introspection, should convince one that there could be no Fallacy of Misplaced Concreteness that mistakes

Entanglement's Challenge to Metaphysics

an aggregate for a whole, if there where no wholes large enough to prehend the aggregate. Actual entities can be of any size; reductionist theories that maintain the only wholes are not complex or not larger than atomic quanta, fail to explain the most obvious aspects of human experiences. Just because the Fallacy of Misplaced Concreteness is often committed by assuming large aggregates are concrete wholes, does not mean all wholes are small. I have argued that metaphysical theory requires wholes of minimal complexity organized in many personal strands to form a lowest-level non-personal society. It also requires a personal society of Wholes of unsurpassable complexity and longevity.

The phenomenon of entanglement, however, seems to be a function of intermediate personal societies, that is, it is a contingent possibility that particles become entangled such that they are not distinguishable as individual personal societies until the entanglement is sufficiently disturbed, at which time one of the entangled possibilities is actualized as an "independent" society. However, all the other entangled particles immediately "collapse" into particles no longer entangled, no matter how far apart they are—tested, so far, to many miles. No transmission time, even at the speed of light, is required, or possible, to cause the simultaneous disengagement (or collapse).

Is this action at a distance? Is this non-contiguous, "spooky" causation? Since the entangled entities can move and remain entangled, the surviving entangled entity would appear to be a personal society of actual occasions that survives some change. Its death is the end of one complex personal society, but is the birth of a separate personal society for each of the entangled entities. Since each moment of the entangled personal society is a whole, when conditions are such that a new entangled whole cannot occur, that is, when the last whole of the entangled society prehends environmental data that is incompatible with its continuance, it collapses. No transmission is required within the whole since what affects any aspect of a whole affects it all simultaneously.

The difficulty of explaining entanglement's disentanglement while requiring all causation to be local, that is, from the result of an occasion to a successive and contiguous occasion, stems from the necessity to posit wholes that can be spatially enormous yet seem to be composed of relatively low-level societies.

One of the principles guiding process thinking is the independence of process from additional causal conditioning once an actual entity is established. Every process whole is caused, or conditioned, by its initial data and its physical base (its given parts), but no new physical input is possible once the actual entity is underway. Process is mentality generating new feelings that must be somewhat like the feelings given to it by its physical base and somewhat different (Category E5, d and e). Mentality is the wholeness of feeling, or the feeling of wholeness: the feeling of the simultaneous all-togetherness of all its parts, something only possible if the whole is more than its parts (Category E9). Mentality is the coming-to-be of a new being containing the beings it begins with. An actual entity is fully windowed as it begins, but fully closed to new data from without once begun, which is the only way to insure the subjective aim, the basis for subjective unity of the actual entity, remains the same throughout its temporal life.

In an entanglement situation, the *processes* of the occasions of two or more personal societies seem to be interacting with each other. It is usually the case that only one new insipient whole starts from the satisfaction/superject of its predecessor (the privileged datum); in the case of entanglement two or more processes seem to terminate in the initiation of one common successor. So long as the entanglement lasts, a complex personal society exists. No subordinate member in the entanglement can reach a satisfaction without all doing so simultaneously.

Each process subsumed in an entanglement is not independent from the others; in fact, they are so intertwined there is no way to even identify individual particles or their qualities. Only upon their disentanglement must they fulfill conditions that identify them individually as different from the others. Until that moment, they exist as aspects of one personal society each of whose successive occasions is a complex process whose satisfactions do not collapse the entanglement but wherein each occasion in the personal society simply re-establishes the conditions for the next moment to continue the give and take among aspects of the new process. When the environmental conditions are such that the new data it provides for the next nascent complex whole is not compatible with its complex continuance, it dies, failing to fulfill its aim, an aim that tried to include the old entangled situation and the new physical data.

Its death, however, allows or forces the entangled societies to "choose" which properties it will independently fulfill. However, various principles of quantum mechanics impose strict conditions on these "choices." If one acquires a right-handed spin, another must survive with a left-handed spin.

Entanglement's Challenge to Metaphysics

The potential differences each member of the entanglement has are actualized in only one way.

Before the whole disintegrates into its individual members, it has the ability to accept some kinds of environmental data into the members of its personal society without collapsing. It can also be tolerant of its entangled members' diverse spatial vectors that require the new members of its personal society to enlarge to keep the divergently vectored aspects within the same occasions of the personal society that includes the entanglement. So each new whole begins with new or additional spatial inclusiveness as required to maintain a new whole with all its entangled parts. What it newly includes seems to be data from societies that are less complex than itself or any entangled aspect of itself. When it encounters more complex societies, they absorb the entangled subordinates of the entangled society simultaneously as the entangled personal nexus collapses.

Chapter 13

Presentational Immediacy

TRANSMUTATION AND TRUTH

TRUTH IS NOT A metaphysical necessity. What exists as a created being is prehended as it is: What exists as being, *must* be prehended as it is or being has become non-being. Prehension is a dyadic relationship, or more precisely, a dipolarity, where the experiencer contains the experienced, where coming-to-be contains being. Truth, however, is a tertiary relationship that depends on partial ignorance of what exists: When what is prehended as it is, truth is irrelevant or redundant. Truth declares that reality is as it asserts it to be. But nothing can be as reality is except reality itself, so any thing other than reality itself is an abstraction from full coming-to-be. Truth asserts that some aspects of reality are like the abstraction said to be true of reality. When it is so, the claim is true.

In practice, something that is relatively clearly experienced is referred to something that is complex or vaguely experienced. In Whitehead's terms, Casual Efficacy is what is experienced or prehended as it is; Presentational Immediacy is a simplified workup of some aspects of Casual Efficacy, usually by way of a lengthy event of occasions in a personal society. To assume that reality is fully what is clearly presented immediately is to commit the Fallacy of Misplaced Concreteness because one is assuming an abstraction, a simplification of the welter of data prehended as an actual occasion begins, is what is concretely real. Symbolic Reference is the tertiary relationship

Presentational Immediacy

asserting the symbol is (in some ways) like that symbolized. Error only occurs when the symbol is assumed to be fully concrete, or when the creative enhancements during a process (particularly, Transmutation) are taken to be identical to the beings inherited at the initiation of the process.

Symbolic Reference is an activity denied of the cosmically inclusive Person, since nothing can be partially or vaguely prehended by the Unsurpassable Personal Society. Divinity can, however, experience the experiences of other occasions' simplifications and symbolic behaviors. Neither is the simplification of Presentational Immediacy an activity of the lowest-level society. Intermediately complex societies may develop "appearance" or simplified awareness that is not exactly as the superjective world of being is. "This 'appearance' is always a perception in the mode of presentational immediacy" (*PR* 329). This happens because one confuses (in the manner of Leibniz's monads) many similar data aspects of subordinate monads as if they where one, a process Whitehead calls "Transmutation." One should be aware that Transmutation cannot be a metaphysical Category, which is the reason it is being discussed in this section on contingent conditions.

The test of truth, when one can't be omniscient of both the symbol and that symbolized, is pragmatic: Action taken in light of the symbol provides expected feedback as new data for some member(s) of the personal society. If actions generate what is expected, one assumes the reference is true. Natural selection will eliminate actions wrong enough to kill the society or put it at a competitive disadvantage. All symbolic reference is "local," that is within one whole (or a personal society of wholes), but it projects its local experience onto a non-local region. The local whole contains coordinate relationships, or what Whitehead calls a "strain locus" (*PR* 319).

The simultaneous experience of coordinate relationships exhibits boundaries or lines definable by extensive relationships apart from any actual content.[12] These lines act as projectors to non-local, and presumably contemporaneous, events. Though Whitehead makes a point of not identifying the definition of a strain locus with the coordination of the simultaneous prehensions of many inputs of the occasion's initial datum (its "duration"), there is a relationship between the two or the possibility

---

12. "A strain-locus is defined by the 'projectors' which penetrate any one finite region within it. Such a locus is a systematic whole, independently of the actualities which may atomize it. In this it is to be distinguished from a 'duration' which does depend on its *physical content*. A strain locus depends merely upon its *geometrical content*" (*PR* 330). "In *The Concept of Nature* these two loci were not discriminated, namely, durations and strain loci" (*PR* 128, footnote).

for truth would be impossible. In the workup from the initial datum to the experience of presentational immediacy, simplification occurs, and even substitutions of one quality for another, but if there were not major similarities or identities, between the two modes of prehension, particularly in the inherited geometrical relationships, the isolation of a personal society within a body would be too haphazard, that is, pathological, to be maintained.

Appendix
The Bare Categoreal Scheme

The Category of the Ultimate Dipolarity and the three types of metaphysical sub-Categories are:

1. The Category of Ultimate Dipolarity
2. Categories of Dipolar Epochal Universality
3. Categories of Dipolar Modal Contrasts
4. Categories of Entity Types and Societal Organization

1. THE CATEGORY OF THE ULTIMATE DIPOLARITY BETWEEN A WHOLE AND ITS PARTS

U: **Each of many wholes that** *comes to be* **is a part in many wholes.**

U_1: Every whole that comes to be is a part in successive wholes forever.

U_2: Every whole that comes to be includes some or all of those that have come to be.

U_3: Every whole that comes to be is a "privileged" part in its immediately successive whole.

U_4: Every whole in striving to come to be either fails, happens to succeed, or necessarily succeeds as peerless.

2. PRINCIPLES OF DIPOLAR EPOCHAL UNIVERSALITY: NECESSITIES EXHIBITED BY *ALL* ACTUAL ENTITIES AT INITIATION AND THROUGHOUT THEIR CREATIVE PROCESSES.

E1: Becomings include beings: Creating includes created.

E1a: Transition from one coming-to-be, as a determinate accomplishment in a successor, is extensionless and unavoidable.

E1b: What has come to be is in successive processes, not in the process that created it.

E1c: Each process is finite in temporal extension. All creative processes cease.

E2: Wholes include parts.

E2a: Wholes (actual entities) are fully "windowed": At their birth they must include all of all prior and contiguous beings.

E2b: Parts, though distinguishable, are not separable.

E2c: Each process is a whole that includes many beings as determinate parts.

E2d: One new part (Being) is common to all new process wholes.

E3: Subjects include objects.

[E3a: Subjectivity is the significance of the present for itself.

E3b: Subjectivity is temporally finite.

E3c: Every object retains its objective self-identity forever.

E3d: Contrasting objects retain their objective diversity forever.

E4: The Present includes the past.

E4a: Past accomplishments are parts of present comings-to-be.

E4b: Distant past accomplishments are parts of parts . . . (and so on) of the present.

E5: The Present includes the future.

E5a: The subject's specific aim is the most specific factor common to all simultaneously inherited beings.

E5b: The objective aim is the common denominator of all possible aims.

E5c: All generic potentiality is carried by the specific aim.

E5d: The future is partly determined by its necessary inclusion of the changeless past and partly open to new creative addition.

E6: The specific aim includes what-ought-to-be.

E6a: What ought-to-be is a subset of what might-be.

E6b: What ought-to-be is a range of co-equally valuable possibilities.

E6c: The ultimate meaning of "value" is a factor in every possible fact describing how every possible actuality must make a difference.

E7: The Evaluator includes the evaluated. Evaluation is always a comparison of parts in a whole to the whole.

E8: Order includes disorder.

E8a: Disorder is always localized within a larger order.

E8b: Inherited disorder is what makes each specific aim unique.

E8c: The possibility for tragedy (and evil) is not preventable.

E9: Freedom includes causation.

E9a: An environment, namely, contiguous, determinate pasts conditioning the present, is unavoidable for every actuality.

E9b: Freedom requires causal conditioning to provide its opportunities.

E10: The novelty of process includes permanence.

E10a: What an actual entity creates is changelessly and everlastingly maintained in others.

E10b: Characteristics found in all possible actualities are "eternal," that is, primordial (never to be found in a first moment exhibiting them) and everlasting (never to be found in a last moment).

E11: Life includes death.

E11a: The "death" (satisfaction) of a moment is included in the inception of other, superseding lives.

E11b: The death of a person, that is, the failure of a personal society to add a new determination, is felt by other lives contiguous to where it would have occurred.

E12: Temporal extension includes spatial extension.

E12a: Relations among contemporary *processing* wholes cannot be experienced. If they are simultaneously objectified (no longer processing) in a superseding whole extending over them, they indicate how they were related as prior processing wholes.

E12b: A temporal extension's satisfaction is included as one of many mutually externally related parts in successive processes that inherit the being. Mutually externally related parts exhibit spatial expansion.

E12c: External relations amongst contemporary *processing* wholes cannot be experienced until they are simultaneously objectified in superseding wholes.

E13: Extensive quantity includes quality.

E13a: A subjective wholes' extensive duration creates new qualities.

E13b: Each whole's termination is a finite, determinate quantity of one or more inherited, and newly specified, qualities.

E13c: An objectified actual entity is a finite quantity of many qualities.

3. PRINCIPLES OF MODAL CONTRAST: MODAL DIPOLAR CATEGORIES CONTRASTING CONDITIONAL AND UNCONDITIONAL WHOLES AT BIRTH AND DURING GROWTH

Modal Categories of Quantity and Perspective: Saving Value at Transition

Transitions from the multiplicity of determinate accomplishments to new creative efforts at each moment consist of one non-perspectival and many perspectival actual entities.

M1: At every Moment one Supreme, Non-perspectival Whole

The Bare Categoreal Scheme

includes all *Satisfied* Perspectival Wholes:

M1a: Spatial all-inclusiveness—Every fragmentary whole's accomplishment is a part of the next all-inclusive Whole.

M1b: Each supreme Whole exhibits all spatiality. (Space expands as new beings are created and simultaneously contrasted with others.)

M1c: Each non-perspectival Whole's epochal rate is unsurpassed in rapidity, but never instantaneous.

M1d: Supreme Wholes' satisfaction/superjects are causally ubiquitous. At each moment, one and only one Being, is contiguous to all new wholes.

and

M2: Many fragmentary, perspectival wholes.

M2a: Each perspectival whole will include all actualizations created prior and contiguous to it, which must always include the latest supreme Creation.

M2b: Each fragmentary whole will exclude some of the actualized entities, namely, those not directly prior and contiguous.

M2c: Many fragmentary wholes are always in process together maintaining prior fragmentary accomplishments.

Modal Categories of Quality and Growth: Creating Value during Process

The multiplicity of contemporaneous creative efforts in process together consists of one supreme Whole and many conditional wholes.

M3: One supreme Whole whose quality of creative effort is always successful and unsurpassed,

M3a: Every supreme Whole's creative effort begins immediately upon completion of the prior Whole in the unsurpassable personal nexus: Process, is continuous, though it is not an actual entity on its own without its dipolar determinate base.

M3b: All creations by all prior fragmentary wholes and non-fragmentary Wholes are felt with complete clarity by each supreme Whole's subjective process.

M3c: Every supreme Whole will terminate in a new determination of unsurpassed value that is the "privileged" part in the next supreme Whole.

and

M4: Some conditional wholes must create qualified values.

M4a: Perspective is a necessary qualification of the value that fragmentary occasions can feel and create.

M4b: Clarity is always qualified, never complete for perspectival actualities.

M4c: The temporal durations of fragmentary wholes must last longer than those of cosmic Wholes.

M4d: Every successful actual occasion is the "privileged" part in the next occasion of a personal nexus.

M4e: The establishment of a new fragmentary occasion (that is more complex than the lowest complexity possible), may fail to create a new being, that is, fail to create a new determinate specification.

M4f: The death of a personal series of moments is the failure of the last moment of the series to create a new determination.

4. ENTITY TYPES AND PRINCIPLES OF SOCIAL ORGANIZATION: CATEGORIES OF NECESSARY CONTRASTS WITHIN PROCESS WHOLES

S1: Actual Entities

S2: Multiplicities

S2a: A process multiplicity is a nexus of contemporary actual entities as they are coming to be (in "unison of becoming"). No actuality can experience this multiplicity while its members are in process.

S2b: The contrasts of beings within an actual entity: (1) Contrasts of simultaneously inherited beings (spatiality). (2) Contrasts of successively related beings (parts within parts, i.e., temporality as change, not process).

S3: Metaphysical principles ("eternal" objects).

S4: Contingent conceptual objects—always more or less indefinite or generic (some or other are necessary in addition to the completely generic Metaphysical Principles).

S4a: Newly created conceptual objects (compare Whitehead's "Reversion").

S4b: Conceptual object contrasting with inherited, subordinate "physical," that is, determinate, objects (the subjective aim).

S4c: Conceptual objects contrasting with conceptual objects (basis of freedom of choice).

S4d: Conceptual object rendered determinate. The transition from conceptual object to determinate being is the transition from one actual entity to another.

S5: Societies

S5a: The unsurpassable, necessary personal society or Individual.

S5b: The lowest-level, necessary, non-personal society.

S5c: Contingent societies: realm of empirical science.

Works Cited

Hartshorne, Charles. *Anselm's Discovery: A Re-Examination of the Ontological Proof for God's Existence*. La Salle, IL: Open Court, 1965.
———. *Creative Synthesis and Philosophic Method*. La Salle, IL: Open Court, 1970.
Whitehead, Alfred North. *Adventures of Ideas*. 1933. New York: Free Press, 1967.
———. *Modes of Thought*. 1938. New York: Free Press, 1968.
———. *Process and Reality: An Essay in Cosmology*. 1929. Corrected edition edited by David Ray Griffin and Donald W. Sherburne. New York: Free Press, 1978.

Index

absolute nothingness, 64
absolute space, 114
abstractions, xvi, xvii, 31
acceleration, 114, 117–20
accumulated contrast, 35
acts of God, 87
acts of nature, 87
actual entity
    anatomy of, 40–42
    contrasts within process wholes, 92–93
    creativity and, 49–51
    death and, 106
    determination and, 6
    dipolarity between a whole and it's parts, 43–45, 135
    initial datum and theory of relativity, 45–47
    metaphysical characteristics, 1
    non-fragmentary, 108
    potentiality and the subjective aim, 47–49
    privileged, 127–28
    relativity and the subjective aim, 52–54
    species of, 22–23
    structured qualities as initial data, 51–52
    subjectivity and the subjective aim, 54–56
    term usage, 4
    units of process, 29–30
    unsurpassability and, 4n1
    See also wholes
actual occasions, 29–30
actualities, 4
actualized whole, 12
Adventures of Ideas (Whitehead), 40–41, 42
agnosticism, 76–77
all-inclusiveness, 78–80
Anaxagoras, 45, 46
animal body, 116
Anselm, 76–77
Anselmian principle, 77
appearance, 133
Aristotle, 8
arrangement, 112
atheism, 76–77
atomism, 31, 56

become, meaning of, 43–44
becoming
    include beings, 10–11, 136
    meaning of, 7
being
    becomings include, 10–11, 136
    chain of, 66
    classes of, 79
    in relation of, 7–8
    Whitehead on, 80–81
Big Bang, 114
birth and death of hierarchal relationships, 101–11
bodies, 101–4
body, moving of, 115–16
brain, 116–17
Buddhists, concrete wholeness, xviii

Index

categoreal obligation
  category of conceptual reversion, 20, 32, 61, 141
  category of conceptual valuation, 11, 58–61
  category of freedom and determination, 15, 18, 63
  category of objective identity and diversity, 13–14, 58, 136
  category of subjective harmony, 13, 16, 61–62
  category of subjective intensity, 63
  category of subjective unity, 11, 28, 39, 57–58, 104–5
  category of transmutation, 13–14, 27, 61, 65, 132–34
categoreal scheme
  about, ix–xii, 5–6
  dipolar epochal universality, 9–21, 136–38
  dipolar modal contrast, 5, 21–28
  dipolar modal principles, 21–28
  entity types, 28–35, 140–41
  epochal universality principle, 9–21, 36–39
  social organization principles, 28–35
  societal organization, 5, 28–35
  ultimate dipolarity, 4, 6–9, 135
  ultimate principle, 6–9
category conceptual reproduction, 58
category of conceptual reversion, 20, 32, 61
category of conceptual valuation, 11, 58–61
category of existence, 29, 31
category of explanation, x, 7, 10–14, 17–18, 20–21, 23–25, 27, 29–35, 42
category of freedom and determination, 15, 18, 63
category of objective diversity, 13–14, 58, 136
category of objective identity, 13, 58
category of obligation, 13–16, 18, 20, 27, 28, 32
category of subjective harmony, 13, 16, 61–62
category of subjective intensity, 14, 15, 63
category of subjective unity, 11, 28, 39, 57–58, 104–5
category of the ultimate, ix–x, 1, 6–9, 10, 43–45, 66, 67, 106
  See also ultimate dipolar principle
category of transmutation, 13–14, 27, 61, 65
causal efficacy, 127, 132
causal ubiquity, 24
causation, condition for freedom, 18, 137
central monad, 103
central personal society, 103
chain of being, 66
change
  actual entity and, 65
  endurance through, 77
  explanation of, 112–14
  meaning of, 1
  metaphysis and, 36–39
chaos theory, 63n8
classical theism, 78
complete determinism, xvii
concepts, 84
conceptual objects, 31–33
conceptual reproduction, 58
conceptual reversion, 20, 32, 61
conceptual valuation, 11, 58–61
concrescence, 13, 45, 53, 70, 95
concrete explanations, xvi–xviii
concrete universal, xviii
concrete whole, 6–7
conditioning process, being as, 10–11
consciousness, 64, 102
contemporary processing, 20
contingent, necessities in, 94–95
contingent complexity, 109–11
contingent conceptual objects, 141
contingent individuals, 34
contingent parts, of wholes, 8
contingent principle of organization, 13
contingent principles, 3
contrasts
  actual entity and, 93–94
  of contrasts, 35
  objects and, 136

Index

coordinate contrasts within process wholes, 92–96
coordinate structure, past as, 95–96
coordinately many, 6
cosmic actual entities, 4n1
cosmic simultaneity and relativity, 80–82
cosmic unity, 82n9
cosmic wholes, 24, 48, 99n10
cosmological theory, 74
created
    conceptual objects, 31–33
    and determinate objects, 33
created beings, 7
creative processes, 64, 73
creativity, 41–44, 49–51, 60

death and dying, 11, 19, 57, 65, 104–9, 137–38
Democritus, 81
determinate specifications, 32–33
determination, xviii–xix, 6, 21, 65
    See also Category of Freedom and Determination
dipolar epochal universality, 9–21, 136–38
dipolar explanations
    epochal foundation, 1
    freedom and determinism, xviii–xix
    inclusive/included pole, xviii
    truth and, xvi
dipolar modal contrast principles
    about, 21–23, 138–40
    quality and growth, 25–28, 139–40
    quantity and perspective, 23–25, 138–39
dipolar whole, 1, 41, 41n5, 135
dipolarity
    described, 4
    between a whole and it's parts, 43–45, 135
dipolarity well, xix
disorder includes order, 17, 137
distant past accomplishments, 14
distinguishable, but not separable, parts, 12
divinity, 86, 133
    See also God

dual transcendence, 82

egoism, 85
Einstein, Albert, 81, 120, 121–22, 126–27
empirical science, xvi
empirically based theism, 76–77
empty space, 64
enduring living objects, 64
enduring non-living objects, 64
enduring objects with conscious knowledge, 64
energy, 122–25
entanglement, 6n3, 8n4, 127–31
entity, metaphysical characteristics, 1
entity types, 28–35, 140–41
epochal categories, 75
epochal foundation
    described, 1
    epochal theory of time, 2
    modal contrasts, 2
    social contrasts, 3
    temporal lifespan, 2
    whole, meaning of, 2–3
epochal universality principle
    about, 9–10
    being, becomings and, 10–11, 136
    evaluators, 16, 137
    finite temporal extension process, 11
    freedom includes causation, 18, 137
    life includes the death, 19, 137–38
    metaphysis and change, 36–39
    order includes disorder, 17, 137
    present includes future, 14–15, 136–37
    process's novelty includes permanence, 18–19, 137
    quantity includes quality, 20–21, 138
    specific aim, 15–16
    subjects include objects, 12–14
    temporal and spatial extension, 19–20
    transition, 10
    wholes include parts, 11–12
error, 133
eternal, 9
eternal objects, 31, 52
eternality, 19

147

Index

evaluators include evaluated, 16, 137
everlasting, 9
everlastingness, 18–19
evil, 17, 72, 90–91
explanations, xv–xvi
extensionless, 10, 109, 136
external objects, 31, 141

fallacy of misplaced concreteness, 4, 35, 67, 121, 124, 127, 128–29, 132
feeling, 58, 60–62, 93
final realities, 29
finite temporal extension process, 11
force, 116
fragment of reality, 23
fragmentary (surpassed) actualities, 4
fragmentary occasion, 28, 55, 55n6, 107–8
fragmentary wholes, 24–25, 139
freedom
   determinism and, xviii–xix
   includes causation, 18, 137
   See also Category of Freedom and Determination
fully-windowed monads, 11–12, 136
future
   present included in, 14–15, 136–37
   relevant, 14, 16
future value, 87

general relativity, 113, 119–20
generic aim of process, 49
God
   Anselm on, 76–77
   attributes of, 86, 87
   nature of, 22, 24–25
   proof of, 65
   veneration of, 83
   Whitehead and, 64
   See also divinity
God/dess, 9, 45, 50, 56, 78, 82–83
good, meaning of, 72
growth and quality, 25–28, 139–40

Hartshorne, Charles
   Anselmian principle, 77
   divine creations, 55
   dual transcendence, 82
   on existence and actuality, 78
   on fragment, 38, 60
   metaphysics definition, 75
   modality, 22
   principle of inclusive contrast, xix
   trichotomy of What, That and How, 76
hate, 89–90
Heraclitus, 36
hierarchal relationships
   about, 101–2
   bodies, 102–4
   contingent complexity, 109–11
   death, 104–9
highest-level personal society, 108

immortality, 45
inclusive contrast principle, xix
individuals as persons, 33–34
inertia, 118–19
ingression, 20–21
inherited objects, 32
initial datum
   structured qualities as, 51–52
   theory of relativity and, 45–47, 51–52
inorganic entities, 68
irrelevance, 80

James, William, 2

Leibniz, 11, 27, 133
life cycle of an actual entity, 41
life includes the death, 19, 137–38
life-line, 100
lifespan, temporal, 2
locality, 126–27
Locke, John, 105
Lorentz's transformation formulas, 113
love, 84–87
lowest-level society, 104, 108–9
low-level, non-personal society, 105–6

many become one, ix, 6, 9, 43–44, 105
mass and acceleration, 117–20, 124
maximally creative processes, 73
measurement, 120–22
metaphysical speculation, 73–74

Index

metaphysics
    actual entities, 1
    change and, 36–39
    explanations and, xvi
    ontological and logical, 21, 75
minimally creative processes, 64
modal categories
    contrasts, 2
    of quality and growth, 25–28, 139–40
    of quantity and perspective, 23–25
modal contrasts, 2, 138–40
modal dipolarity, 4
modal necessities, 75
modal principles, 2, 3
modality, 22
moment
    actualities, 4
    of reality, 3–4
monads
    central, 103
    fully-windowed, 11–12, 136
    Leibniz on, 133
    peephole, 11–12
    windowless, 11, 59
motion
    change of spatial position, 114
    transition versus, 99–100
movement, 112–15
moving society, 115–17
multiple fragmentary creations, 25
multiplicities, 30–31, 140

natural selection, 133
necessary, coordinate contrasts within process wholes
    actual entity, 92–93
    in the contingent, 94–95
    contrasts, 93–94, 140–41
    past as coordinate structure, 95–96
necessary aspects, of wholes, 8, 140–41
necessary existence, 65
necessary existing society
    of non-perspectival occasions, 73–91
    of perspectival occasions, 64–72
necessary individual, 34
necessity as societal function, 64–67
negative, being, 87

negative prehension, 11–12, 27, 46, 59
non-determinate specifications, 32
non-fragmentary actual entity, 108
non-local influence, 126
non-moving wholes
    energy, 122–25
    mass and acceleration, 117–20
    measurement, 120–22
    movement, 112–15
    moving society, 115–17
non-personal societies, 65, 73–74, 103–4, 106
non-perspectival occasions, necessary existing society of
    about, 73–78
    all-inclusiveness, 78–80
    evil, 90–91
    hate, 89–90
    love, 84–87
    maximally creative process, 73
    positive value, 88
    relativity and cosmic simultaneity, 80–82
    unsurpassable quality, 82–84
nothingness, xvii, 64, 67–68, 90, 124

objective aim, 15, 16, 49–50
objective diversity, 13–14, 58, 136
objective identity, 13
objectively immortal, 74
occasion, fragmentary actualities, 4
one, meaning, 43
ontological principle, 25–26
order includes disorder, 17, 137

pantheism
    concrete universal, xviii
    as multiplicity of contemporaneous and successive substances, 9
    structure of reality, 31
pantheisms, as solipsism, 91
Parmenides, xviii, 36–37, 47
partially determinate future, 15
partially open future, 15
part-whole language, 4n2
past
    as coordinate structure, 95–96
    present included in, 14, 136

Index

past *(continued)*
  as sequential, 95–96
past accomplishments, 14
peephole monads, 11–12
perishing, 59
permanence, 18–19, 137
personal order, 70–71, 101
personal society, 28, 102–3, 105
persons, individuals as, 33–34
perspectival exclusions, 25
perspectival inclusions, 25
perspectival occasions
  minimally creative processes, 64
  necessary existing society of, 64–72
  necessity as societal function, 64–67
  subordinate pole, 67–71
  value theory, 71–72
perspectival whole, 23–24
perspective, 60
perspective, quantity and, 23–25, 138–39
philosophical explanation, xv
philosophical inquiry, xv
philosophy, Whitehead on, xviii
Planck, Max, 127
Plato, 37, 82
points, 120
positive prehension, 12
positive value, 88
possibilities, value dimension of, 16
potentiality
  actualization of, 51
  being and, 61
  as a continuum, 80
  meaning of, 18
  pure, 15, 18, 48
  real, 18, 41, 48
  and the subjective aim, 47–49
prehended multiplicities, 31
prehension, theory of, 3
present
  includes future, 14–15, 136–37
  includes past, 14, 136
  significance of, 13
presentational immediacy, 14, 121, 127, 132–34
primordial, 9, 19
principle, Anselmian, 77

principle, ontological, 25–26
principle, ultimate, 6–9
  See also category of the ultimate
principle of dipolar modal contracts.
  See dipolar modal contrast principles
principle of epochal universality. *See* epochal universality principle
principle of inclusive contrast, xix
principle of organization, 13
principle of reality, 59
principles, modal, 2, 3
principles of social organization
  about, 28–29
  actual entities, 29–30
  contrasts of contrasts, 35
  created, conceptual objects, 31–33
  created and determinate objects, 33
  entity types and, 140–41
  eternal objects, 31
  individuals as persons, 33–34
  multiplicities, 30–31, 140
privileged actual entities, 127–28
privileged beginning, 6
privileged object, 13
privileged part, 27
privileged successor, 6, 105
process, defined, 7
Process and Reality (Whitehead), 5, 42
process determination, 6
process multiplicities, 30
processes, permanence and, 18–19, 137
Proslogium (Anselm), 76
pure potentiality, 15, 18, 48

qualitatively diverse values, 6
qualities, 20
quality
  growth and, 25–28, 139–40
  quantity and, 20–21, 138
  unsurpassable, 82–84
quantity and perspective, 23–25, 138–39
quantum mechanics, 81–82

radiation, 114–15
rational schema, 1
rationalism, xvii

Index

real, term usage, 41
real potentiality, 18, 41, 48
reality, xvi
reality principle, 59
rearrangement, 112
relativism, xvii
relativity
   experiences and, 112
   general, 113, 119–20
   special, 113, 118
   subjective aim and, 52–54
   theory of, 45–47, 81–82, 126–27
relativity and cosmic simultaneity, 80–82
relevant future, 14, 16
revenge, 91
revision, 61

schisms, xv–xvi
sequential contrasts within process wholes, 97–100
sequentially many, 6
simultaneous, coordinate contracts, 33
social categories, 3
social contrasts, 3
social organization principles. *See* principles of social organization
societal function, necessity as, 64–67
societal inclusiveness, 6
societal longevity, 6
societies, 4, 141
Socrates, 82
solipsism, 91
space, 94, 112, 114, 120
spatial all-inclusiveness, 24
spatial expansiveness, 24
spatial extension, 2, 19–20, 52, 123, 138
spatial multiplicities, 33
spatial position, 114
spatiality, 19–20
spatial-temporal continuum, 120
spatial-temporal omniscience, 24
special relativity, 113, 118
specific aim, 14, 15–16, 137
specific difference, 74
specifications, 20–21
spin, 124
spooky action, 126, 129

stability, 18
straightness, 120
strain locus, 133, 133n12
structured qualities as initial data, 51–52
subjective aim
   creativity and, 49–51
   potentiality as, 47–49
   relativity and, 52–54
   subjectivity and, 54–56
subjective experience, 1
subjective intensity, 14, 15, 63
subjectivity, 13, 54–56, 136
subjects include objects, 12–14, 136
subordinate pole, 67–71
successive contrasts, 33
successor, 6, 105, 106, 106n11
suffering, 91
supreme (unsurpassed) actualities, 4, 23
supreme wholes, 2, 5, 23–27
surpassed (fragmentary) actualities, 4
surpassed clarity, 27
symbolic reference, 127, 132–33

temporal duration, 27
temporal epoch, 3
temporal lifespan, 2
temporal multiplicities, 33
temporal omniscience, 24
temporal order, 70
temporal sequence, 112
temporality, 20
temporally extension, 1–2, 10, 19–20, 123, 138
temporally extensionless, 10
temporally finite subjectivity, 13
theism, classical, 78
theory of prehension, 3
theory of relativity, 45–47, 81–82
time, 77, 113
tragedy is not preventable, 17
transcendence, dual, 82
transformation formulas, Lorentz, 113
transition
   motion versus, 99–100
   saving value at, 23
   as temporally extensionless, 10

Index

transition *(continued)*
   term usage, 44
   universals and, 98–99
   Whitehead and, 58–59
transmutation, 3, 13–14, 27, 61, 65, 132–34
trichotomy of What, That and How, 76
truth and truths, xvii, 132, 133–34

ultimate aim, 15, 16
ultimate dipolar principle, 4, 6–9, 135
   See also category of the ultimate
ultimate principle, 6–9
   See also category of the ultimate
ultra-rationalism, xvii
unconditional whole, 26, 138–40
universals, transition and, 98–99
unsurpassability, 4n1, 71, 83, 86
unsurpassable level of personally ordered, 71
unsurpassable personal nexus, 26, 71
unsurpassable quality, 82–84
unsurpassed (supreme) actualities, 4
unsurpassed value, 26, 27

value
   future, 87
   meaning of, 16, 137
   positive, 88
   qualified, 27
   state of, 78
   unsurpassed, 26
value dimension of possibilities, 16
value theory, 71–72

what-ought-to-be, 15–16, 137
Whitehead
   actual entity, 52, 54
   Adventures of Ideas, 40–41, 42
   atomism, 56
   on being, 80–81
   on categories, 2
   category of freedom and determination, 63
   category of obligation, 28
   category of subjective unity, 28, 104–5
   causal efficacy, 132
   change, 36, 39
   concrescence, 53
   creativity, 37
   cyclical nature of temporal extension, 1–2
   determinate parts each whole simultaneously, 2
   eternal objects, 15
   external objects, 31, 141
   fallacy of misplaced concreteness, 4
   feelings, 61
   God and, 22, 25, 64
   on God/dess, 9
   ingression, 21
   inorganic entities, 68
   life cycle of an actual entity, 41
   many become one, 43–44
   metaphysical speculation, 73–74
   on nature of God, 22, 25
   negative prehension, 11–12, 46, 59
   one, meaning of, 43
   personal order, 70
   on philosophy, xviii
   potentiality, 61
   prehension of actual entities, 34
   principle, all are on the same level, 10
   principle of reality, 59
   Process and Reality, 5, 42
   species of actual entities, 22
   specific difference, 74
   straightness, 120
   strain locus, 133, 133n12
   subjective forms, 52
   theory of prehension, 3
   transition, 58–59
   transmutation, 133
whole
   concrete, 6–7
   dipolar, 1, 41, 41n5, 135
   meaning of, xviii–xix, 2–3, 7–8, 23
   unconditional, 26, 138–40
wholes
   actual entity and, 92–93
   contingent parts, 8
   cosmic, 24, 48, 99n10
   fragmentary, 24–25, 139
   include parts, 11–12, 136

Index

necessary aspects, 8, 140–41
non-moving (*See* non-moving wholes)
perspectival, 23–24
supreme (*See* supreme wholes)

See also actual entity
windowless monads, 11, 59

Zeno's paradox, 127